Getting Started with .NET Aspire

Build Cloud-Native and Distributed Applications with Ease

Dave Rael

Apress®

Getting Started with .NET Aspire: Build Cloud-Native and Distributed Applications with Ease

Dave Rael
Denver, CO, USA

ISBN-13 (pbk): 979-8-8688-1520-1   ISBN-13 (electronic): 979-8-8688-1521-8
https://doi.org/10.1007/979-8-8688-1521-8

Copyright © 2025 by Dave Rael

Managing Director, Apress Media LLC: Welmoed Spahr
Acquisitions Editor: Ryan Byrnes
Editorial Assistant: Gryffin Winkler

Cover designed by eStudioCalamar

Cover image designed by Pexels

Distributed to the book trade worldwide by Springer Science+Business Media New York, 1 New York Plaza, New York, NY 10004. Phone 1-800-SPRINGER, fax (201) 348-4505, e-mail orders-ny@springer-sbm.com, or visit www.springeronline.com. Apress Media, LLC is a Delaware LLC and the sole member (owner) is Springer Science + Business Media Finance Inc (SSBM Finance Inc). SSBM Finance Inc is a **Delaware** corporation.

For information on translations, please e-mail booktranslations@springernature.com; for reprint, paperback, or audio rights, please e-mail bookpermissions@springernature.com.

Apress titles may be purchased in bulk for academic, corporate, or promotional use. eBook versions and licenses are also available for most titles. For more information, reference our Print and eBook Bulk Sales web page at http://www.apress.com/bulk-sales.

Any source code or other supplementary material referenced by the author in this book is available to readers on GitHub. For more detailed information, please visit https://www.apress.com/gp/services/source-code.

If disposing of this product, please recycle the paper

This book is dedicated to the memory of my father, Pat Rael, who was the best role model I could have ever had for being a dad, husband, and serious professional. Your competence, kindness, and giving spirit were exemplary. Your example, support, and love made me who I am. You departed this life too soon during the writing of this book, and I can't get used to the idea that you're gone. I miss you and I always will.

Table of Contents

About the Author

Dave Rael is a father, husband, real estate investor, and seasoned software professional. He has worked as a software developer, analyst, tester, engineer, and architect in numerous verticals and industries over the course of more than 25 years. In 1999, he started in professional software development for a large telecom company working with C++ and Visual Basic and began .NET and C# development in the early .NET Beta releases. Though dabbling in Java, Ruby, Go, Node, and various other languages and platforms, .NET has remained his home and primary source of coding joy, especially with enthusiasm rekindled by the introduction of .NET Core, which enabled .NET development and runtime on platforms other than only Windows.

About the Technical Reviewer

 **Gerald Versluis** is a senior software engineer at Microsoft working on .NET MAUI. Since 2009, Gerald has been working on a variety of projects ranging from frontend to backend and everything in between, which involve C#, .NET, Azure, ASP.NET, and all kinds of .NET technologies. At some point, he fell in love with cross-platform and mobile development with Xamarin, now .NET MAUI. Since that time, he has become an active community member, producing content online and presenting on all things tech at conferences around the globe. Gerald can be found on most social media channels by his handle @jfversluis, blogging at `https://blog.verslu.is`, or on his YouTube channel: `https://youtube.com/@jfversluis`.

Acknowledgments

Writing a book is a task that requires more effort than you'd ever expect. There is individual work, but it's ultimately a team effort. There are many contributors that have gone into bringing this book to life.

I'd like to start with thanking my wife and kids for their support in allowing me space to work and for helping me fix my words that were often not right with the first pass. You are my motivation, my inspiration, and a set of powerful teammates in everything I do.

Thank you to Microsoft and the .NET Aspire team for creating a project worth writing about that really changes the game for the developer experience. I believe Aspire is a revolution in the ways teams onboard new members and carry out the daily work of delivering valuable software. I love what you've done and can't wait to see where you take it going forward.

A special thank you to Gerald Versluis for the outstanding suggestions in the technical review of this book. Your input has made this a much better product than it would have been otherwise. The value you bring is clear.

Thanks also to Apress, especially Ryan Byrnes and Deepa Tryphosa. Thank you for connecting with me and offering this opportunity. Your patience with my life events getting in the way of book progress and your amazing efforts on making this project come to life are unforgettable.

Preface

Microsoft shipped .NET Aspire at the 2024 Build conference and surprised everyone. It got a lot of immediate attention and hype. It created excitement, but also confusion. It's an ambitious project and requires some time to start to understand what problems it solves.

This book aims to help you get up to speed with understanding .NET Aspire. It will help you understand why it exists and what it can do for you. From there, it will help you get started knowing how to use Aspire to make your software development experience better than it was before.

Aspire was created, at least in part, to enable a smoother developer onboarding process in which you can just clone a source repository and run the code without a lot of ceremony. It solves the problem of having to follow multiple documented steps or running scripts and various tools.

A system built with .NET Aspire is composed of different resources working together as a cohesive whole. Some of those resources are processes running your code and others are sourced from elsewhere. All of them need to run, and they need to be discoverable by one another to have a working system.

Simply put, .NET Aspire makes life better for software professionals working on software on their machines. It has more to offer as well, but that's the main piece. This book is a journey in getting acquainted with Aspire, what it is, what it does, and how to get the most from it.

Who This Book Is For

If you are trying to gain an understanding of what .NET Aspire has to offer and if it's for you, this book can help. If you already know you want to use .NET Aspire and need help getting started, you have come to the right place. If you're already using .NET Aspire and are looking for greater understanding or further tips, there's likely something here for you.

This book is intended to be an introductory treatment of getting started with .NET Aspire. If you have already gone beyond merely getting started, there is likely less for you here, but still some information and understanding that can be useful.

The activities should help you to understand not only how to use Aspire, but what it's doing for you so that you become a more powerful user. It will enable you to fit Aspire into your context smoothly.

Introduction

Motivations for .NET Aspire

The Problem for Software

If you embark on the journey of creating a software system, you have a problem.

First and foremost, there's a problem you need to solve. Software is only useful in the context of trying to address a need for a human being. It may not be that this problem is directly your problem. Someone has a problem, and you want to create software to address the problem. It may be the case that the problem is less problem and more opportunity, but still, the term problem covers the ground of somebody needing something software can provide. If you come to an agreement with someone else under which you'll create software to solve their problem, you have adopted their problem as your own. Perhaps more directly, you likely have the problem of needing an income, and making someone else's problem into your own is a way to address that need.

One way or another, you have a problem. You intend to solve your problem, at least in part, with software.

The Problem of Software

Knowing you have a problem and you intend to use software as a remedy, you've addressed the two most important of the fundamental questions: "Why?" and "What?"

The reason you are taking action is articulated as the core problem you're trying to solve. The what is the software system you intend to build. The next question to address becomes the question of "How?"

In the landscape of building software, it seems there are as many choices as there are stars in the sky.

You have a vast array of choices to use with various platforms, toolsets, languages, hosting environments, and more. It can be hard to know where to start.

For the purposes of this book about .NET Aspire, we're going to narrow that field of choices considerably. If you're here and interested in .NET Aspire, you probably already have an interest in the .NET platform and what it has to offer. Even if you're not using .NET as your main implementation platform, Aspire can improve your experience, but it's likely you'll want to use .NET for some of your system. There are many other options, and .NET is not necessarily always the best choice for a given situation, but it is a good, general-purpose platform useful for most technical problems. In many cases, it is, indeed, the best choice to use for your solution. Even in cases where it may not be best, it's almost always at least good enough.

With .NET and C# in hand as the start of from where implementation will proceed, we're not done with the problems of deciding on how to design and build a system. It's a good start, though.

Beyond languages and runtime platforms, choices need to be made about where software will execute and how you will compose your solution.

Among the choices of where to run, the first option that usually comes to mind in modern software development is to use one of the full-service cloud providers that enable developers to focus on the problem of creating software systems and to leave the business of operating server farms to dedicated professionals, working for large companies.

Cloud platforms provide APIs and toolsets that enable the automation of creation and management of resources for serving the needs of any application. They provide flexibility for how you want to work and at what cost.

Running in cloud services is not necessarily always the best place for all systems, but in modern software development, it's a good default choice, enabling elastic scale and straightforward provision of resources at costs that grow only as the needs of the system grow (if designed in ways that take advantage of the nature of the cloud). In most cases, starting in the cloud is the best path and it's viable and perhaps optimal for the longer term as well.

The Problems of the Cloud

Given software that runs in the cloud, the nature of the cloud immediately starts to assert itself as one thinks about system design. Cloud resources are generally best used when specific resources are created and used for specific purposes, leading to systems designed with multiple resources. As opposed to a software application designed to run on a single machine serving all the needs of the application, cloud designs tend toward systems composed of multiple resources all running independently for distinct purposes and enlisted into serving the common purpose of a broader system.

Cloud systems are usually *distributed systems*. Distributed systems typically make use of multiple resources, often addressable in differing ways and using various protocols, interfaces, and ways of interacting. Networking is a first-class part of a distributed system, in addition to the components that need to communicate with one another over networks.

Applications and Systems

Thus, cloud software is usually system software, not simply an application. An application can be thought of as a single process running on a single machine. A system is a federation of multiple processes, typically running on multiple machines and encompassing resources like storage, including database systems.

Systems require orchestration to get the multiple independent parts of the whole to work cohesively together. When designing a software system, it's important to be able to plan for, create, implement, and deploy all the pieces that make up the system in ways that are repeatable to be able to create a working system in a set of environments. It's also important to consider what happens in the case of failure of parts of the system. There is no such thing as system components that are always reliable, and considerations must be made for how the system should behave if any portion of the system is unable to function. Cloud systems must be designed for resilience, fault tolerance, and scalability.

The notion of computing, storage, communication, telemetry, and other resources that can be designed and implemented in repeatable ways and deployed to multiple environments for different purposes, leveraging the capability of the cloud, and responding to changing needs and conditions is the basis for the idea of a "cloud-native" approach.

Cloud Native

Cloud-native approaches and tools ease the burden of software organizations on creating and using the resources made available by cloud providers through specific languages and toolsets for specifying and leveraging needed capabilities. The aim of cloud-native software is to make use of the elastic flexibility of cloud computing providers to build systems that respond effectively to changing needs and work in the face of resources that can be ephemeral. In short, cloud-native software must be flexible in order to take advantage of the flexible offerings of cloud environments.

Cloud-native systems are distributed systems. These systems are composed of multiple pieces comprising various types of resources and deployed software elements, built from source, packaged in reusable bundles, and provisioned from cloud providers to serve system needs.

Using cloud providers makes these types of designs approachable, relative to needing to provision hardware to serve the needs of an organization. There's a bit of a mismatch, though, between what it's like to deploy cloud-native systems in cloud environments compared to running such a system on the workstation of the typical developer.

The Problem of the Developer Workstation

To test software in progress during the writing of the components of a software system, developers use many approaches. The broadest bed of testing is usually that of unit tests that automate execution of small chunks of functionality in the source code of application logic. These tests are important, and they execute relatively quickly and should therefore be numerous. They only address part of the problem, though. Integration tests that test more of the pieces of the software, working together, are also necessary to get a fuller picture of making sure the parts fit together to make a whole. Further still, there's a need for both automated and manual testing of the whole system, running in totality, to make sure that everything works from end to end.

Developers need to be able to execute all these types of tests frequently. Ideally, they should be able to run entire systems completely contained within their workstations.

This can be a bit challenging with a cloud-native approach in which a system makes use of multiple resources enabled by a cloud provider. When a system makes use of many pieces, to have a working environment for testing the system, multiple pieces are required.

This can get complicated for setting up a working system on a developer workstation.

Solutions

Fortunately, there are aids to ease this mismatch of the way we run software in the cloud compared to on workstations. Many cloud providers have used some standards in some of their offerings so that one can run software in standard ways like using containers in many different clouds, as well as on developer workstations. Kubernetes has become the most popular of the offerings for orchestration of workloads in containers and pretty much every cloud provider has support for it. There are many ways of running containers on a workstation, and there are alternatives for managing multicontainer environments and networks, especially on workstations, like Docker Compose. Docker Compose is not necessarily only for the workstation, but it is useful for setting up resources on a workstation and solutions like Kubernetes are generally used for canonical environments.

In a typical organization, software might be developed using a platform like .NET, with the output of building the software packaged into container images by continuous integration pipelines that also execute tests and perform the likes of quality and security scans. These container images might be deployed to canonical environments in Kubernetes clusters by continuous delivery/deployment pipelines with further tests executed in these environments. A Compose file or a set of Compose files might be in place to set up a developer workstation with a running environment, including containerized workloads for the software itself, data stores, caches, secret storage, networking, and other dependencies.

Such a setup is a viable way of managing the needs of development, packaging, testing, and deploying a system. Many organizations have used setups like this with success. Containers have truly changed the landscape of systems development for the better. In fact, tools like Docker and Docker Compose are a breath of fresh air for application and systems developers looking to create reliable software.

There are some problems that remain, though. Orchestration of all these different resources must typically be done independently, at least to an extent, for the cloud and for the developer workstation. This means potentially needing to write and maintain different Kubernetes manifests and/or Helm charts for deployed environments in addition to Docker Compose files for the workstation. Service discovery is also often done differently between the types of environments. Further, observability and instrumentation of what is happening in the independent system components can be hard to track and follow and might need to be done differently in different places.

For these reasons, the situation for modern developers is good and new heights for scalable and reliable systems are achievable, but there is still more to be desired.

The modern developer experience is good in ways we couldn't have imagined a decade or two ago, and it continues to get better.

It's still far from perfect, though. Setting up networks and dependencies with Docker Compose and building images take a finite amount of time when developers want to have their local systems up and running without having to wait and without fuss. It's always harder to set up workstations with all the necessary pieces than it should be in an ideal world. Maintaining separate setups for the workstation in addition to setting up environment deployments is an extra burden we'd rather do without.

Fortunately, .NET developers now have another option for bridging the gap between development and canonical cloud environments.

It's called .NET Aspire.

CHAPTER 1

Introducing .NET Aspire

What Is .NET Aspire?

To deal with the problems inherent in the development of cloud-native distributed systems, Microsoft has introduced a toolset known as .NET Aspire. It takes a little time to get up to speed with understanding what .NET Aspire really is and what problems it solves, but it's worth the commitment.

One of the main sources of friction it addresses is that it's hard to start working on a new project or to add a new team member. New contributors often have sets of instructions to follow just to get to the point of being able to execute the code and run tests. You are often faced with installing tools, running scripts, setting up data, and more. With .NET Aspire in the picture, you'll mostly be able to just acquire source code and execute it. This is an exciting change.

.NET Aspire has .NET right in the name, and it's from Microsoft, which might lead you to believe it's only about .NET. This is not true. Systems using Aspire can run a diverse set of workloads using various platforms and technologies. .NET projects are certainly supported and are usually a key feature of a .NET Aspire system, but you can do a lot more as well.

© Dave Rael 2025
D. Rael, *Getting Started with .NET Aspire*, https://doi.org/10.1007/979-8-8688-1521-8_1

The key characteristic of a system that can benefit from Aspire is that it is distributed. This means that it makes use of more resources than just a single process running on a single machine. In Chapter 4, I'll discuss system architecture and get into the differences between systems and applications. For getting familiar with what Aspire is, know that the use of resources like data stores, in addition to running your code, makes for a simple distributed system. Obviously, system complexity can increase greatly from there.

When you have a distributed system, you have more than one resource to run when you want the software to operate. Running multiple resources is harder than running one. The complexity of distributed systems that require multiple running processes and connected pieces leads to the need to do more than just get the code and run. There are remedies for this with tools for setting up infrastructure, but all of them have limitations. Further, the tools that enable this are often using different languages and formats than the code you use in your domain, so there's more to learn and maintain.

To make matters worse, running multiple dependencies and processes on a developer workstation can lead to the spawning of multiple shell windows and a feeling of loss of control. Also, this leads to difficulty in tracking what is running and what's not and finding the right logs for the right piece necessary to understand any situation.

.NET Aspire enables using .NET code to specify an "application model" that describes your system in a way that it can just run. The primary benefit of this is that you can use a familiar language, like C#, to define a whole system with pieces that may be .NET processes, databases, message queues, storage containers/buckets, Python processes, Node.js/JavaScript/ Typescript applications, or just about anything else you can imagine. A lot of the "anything else you can imagine" is enabled by using containers to run workloads, which gives a lot of flexibility.

When you execute your application model, you execute your system. Aspire also provides a handy dashboard, accessible in your browser, summarizing your resources and providing easy access to configuration, health status, logs, metrics, and traces for each of the resources and for the whole system.

In addition to enabling the construction of an application model that can just run on your workstation with all of the pieces you'll need for your system, it also enables you to standardize the way you structure and implement your service discovery, health checks, and system observability so you can connect your software internally, know what is happening in your system, and address any problems that arise.

Further, .NET Aspire produces a manifest you can use for deployment of your system to canonical environments and environments on demand. You may or may not make use of the manifest produced, especially if you already have a system and you're deploying with Infrastructure as Code, pipelines, and/or GitOps. You have options, though. Chapter 7 will discuss deployment options and some of the available tools that extend the Aspire manifest into real deployment artifacts.

Using project and solution templates, it is straightforward to get started with building systems that are ready for the cloud and modern software development and operations. Aspire begins by enabling a smooth developer experience. It provides support for running a potentially complex system on developer workstations and options for deployment to canonical environments. In short, it's an end-to-end set of tools for designing, building, testing, deploying, operating, observing, and monitoring distributed systems.

The Tools Provided by .NET Aspire

When you use .NET Aspire, whether via the .NET command-line interface, in Microsoft Visual Studio, Visual Studio Code, or with the Aspire support in JetBrains Rider, you get a set of project and solution templates to help with setting up Aspire projects. This includes a template to start from a blank system and fill with your designs, templates for sample systems, and templates for individual project types that can be mixed and matched to build up a system. You can start from scratch to build a new system or add Aspire and its components to existing systems. These templates are useful and provide projects to which you can add functionality, or they can serve as examples to guide you in adding the right packages to your existing or other new projects.

In addition to useful blank starting points and individual project templates, Aspire provides sample templates useful for getting acquainted with how systems built on .NET Aspire are laid out and how the pieces interact with one another. In Chapter 2, we'll look at using the starter solution template as an example to get comfortable with all the pieces, packages, and code necessary.

Most of the magic that happens with .NET Aspire is via NuGet packages you'll reference from your projects. The project templates include these references to get you started quickly.

Elements of a System Built with .NET Aspire

The first thing one might notice when dealing with .NET Aspire is that a system built with Aspire will likely contain projects specific to Aspire systems. Most notably, a project of a type called an app host will likely be present in a system leveraging .NET Aspire. This project serves as an orchestrator for the rest of the processes necessary for running the system.

It's a central element that, when executed, will cause the rest of the setup of the system to run. This is an answer to the pain of developing distributed systems with multiple dependencies.

It can be a chore to start all the necessary processes, databases, transports, and other resources required. In addition to making sure all the right resources run, you need to make certain they are available in the right order so that the dependencies of any given piece are met. The app host project gives a developer a single point to start the whole system, considering the dependencies between them and with options for running as you prefer.

Further, when one starts a .NET Aspire system by using the app host project, another part of the offering comes to immediate attention. With .NET Aspire systems, a dashboard summarizing the various resources is served. Using a standard web browser, you can view the running resources, locate their addresses, and view logs, settings, environment variables, and telemetry. It's a one-stop shop to see what is happening on a running system, and it is provided for you by .NET Aspire with a simple *dotnet run* or a start from Visual Studio or other integrated development environment.

The app host project is at the heart of a .NET Aspire system and is the point of definition for the elements that make up a distributed system. In leveraging the app host project, you can specify multiple projects that run in their own processes in your system and set up dependencies between them such that service discovery can wire them together on your workstation and in deployed environments as well. In addition to your own projects in your solution, you can also leverage other types of workloads, including containers, to run further elements of your system. Some of these are processes you build, while others may be provided by other teams, businesses, or communities.

Another project you're likely to find in a system built on .NET Aspire is the service defaults project. This project is the core of the service discovery built into Aspire. It also sets up telemetry and health checks and is a place to define standards for what you want from your processes for how they surface information about their health and capability.

As a general rule, your app host project will reference the projects where you implement the processes that expose the functionality of your domain, and your .NET projects will reference the service defaults project. Beyond these projects, you'll have references in your AppHost project to packages defining workloads you'll want to reference, some of them likely as containers, like dependencies for databases, caches, message queueing systems, and other resources.

Further, .NET Aspire offers support for testing. Any of the code you author in a .NET Aspire system can be unit tested like any other code without any need for anything from Aspire. There's also support for testing your system more as it will execute, rather than testing units in isolation. Well-tested systems generally make use of tests both running isolated code units in a test runner context and testing by interacting with real system processes and making assertions on system output or system state.

The support for testing provided by .NET Aspire will run your distributed system by running the app host in process during test execution, with support for service discovery from test code, allowing you to make requests against and take actions in your system and make assertions on the resulting outcomes. I'll explore this type of testing with .NET Aspire further in Chapter 5.

In addition to all the above goodness provided by .NET Aspire, there are extensions that facilitate the inclusion of many commonly used services and offerings called *integrations*. These are NuGet packages you can add in your app host and application process projects to incorporate many of the cloud-native resources you might use in a system, like databases, secret stores, identity providers, or any number of different offerings. Integrations are covered in more depth in Chapter 6.

Therefore, the main elements of a .NET Aspire system are the following:

- The system orchestration project, known as the app host

- The service defaults project for setting up service discovery, health checks, telemetry, and any other standards you want in the constituent elements of your system

- Your .NET application process projects

- You other application process projects, like Single Page Application frontends or other projects using other languages and platforms outside .NET

- Workloads referenced as packages known as *integrations*

- Other workloads, authored by you or by others, often leveraged as containers (though not necessarily in containers)

- Test projects, including tests that run against the executing application via .NET Aspire support for integration testing against systems

Reasons Distributed Systems Development Is Better with .NET Aspire Than Without

There are alternatives to .NET Aspire. Many in the cloud-native development world use tools like Docker Compose to be able to create environments on workstations in which systems under development can be executed and tested. Docker Compose is a nice tool to enable creating multiple resources with a single action.

It requires being set up itself, though, and maintenance as you add elements to your system. Maintaining a *Compose file* is not hard, but it's something you must do in addition to setting up your application and the references it has to its dependencies. Compose requires you to set up networking and needs to build container images from your process projects before it can run them. You're also usually maintaining Compose files for workstation execution in addition to manifests, charts, scripts, or other sets of configurations for deploying your application into environments off your workstation.

.NET Aspire enables running systems on your workstation with a single point of having to set them all up. It also provides for service discovery in your C# code in your application so that it will just work on your workstation with a single invocation. Setting up your projects with configuration to know the ports or other addresses on which to reference one another is not hard, but it's something you must do to get distributed systems working and it would be nice if you didn't have to. Aspire can also be used to generate the resources you need for deploying to a variety of types of cloud infrastructure with support for Kubernetes and others. There will be more on what this looks like and how you'll want to use it in Chapter 7.

.NET Aspire makes it straightforward to run systems locally and in the cloud and to get new team members up and running quickly and with a minimum of fuss.

It really makes developing distributed systems a lot easier than it ever was without it.

Without .NET Aspire, you're left with orchestrating and addressing resources on your own with a different set of tools for your workstations than for deployed environments. You've probably had the experience of, on the first day of a new job, trying to compile and run the code in the repository you've just cloned and running into failure after failure because of not having set up the resource that some connection string points at and resolving that just to see the next thing that's still broken. Then you fix that to find the next error. This can be an exercise in pulling out your hair before you finally get to the point of running the software successfully.

With .NET Aspire, you set up the way your system operates once with the familiar tools of .NET projects and C# code and you're able to just run on your workstations. If you need to change the way things operate or the order of start of dependencies or anything of the sort, you do it with a familiar language in a familiar environment and commit it to source control to share with your team.

For these reasons, .NET Aspire is a real win for developers creating modern distributed systems.

Summary

Getting familiar with .NET Aspire is a process that takes some time and effort. It introduces ideas, concepts, and vocabulary you'll need to assimilate. In addition to Aspire-specific ideas, it leverages cloud-native technologies and concepts with their own learning curve. It is daunting to try to understand the many moving parts of the modern software landscape.

Don't worry, though. Software development has always been a moving target and nobody understands everything. There are a lot of ideas and terms to get used to, but you don't need to know everything all at once to start getting value from any toolset, including .NET Aspire. In the rest of this book, I'll help you with understanding what Aspire has to offer and how you can use it to quickly make your life better. Exhaustive coverage of everything you need to know about any sufficiently complex topic is impossible, but I'll give you enough so that you can start moving and know what you need to do to find out more.

This chapter introduced what Aspire is, what it can do for you, and the problem it solves. The next chapter will look at how you can get started with using it, starting with dependencies and installation and then looking at how to use what it provides.

## CHAPTER 2

Getting Started with .NET Aspire

Now that you've seen a little of the problem .NET Aspire is trying to solve, why it exists, and what it is, the next question on your mind is likely that of how to use it. We'll start with installation and then move from there into how to use the tools and what they provide.

Installing the Tools

To get started with using .NET Aspire, the first thing you want to do is install some tools. Technically, you don't really have to do this. Most of .NET Aspire is delivered via NuGet packages that you could reference from projects you could create from scratch. However, the .NET Aspire tooling, when installed, is extremely helpful in setting up the types of projects you'll want with the package references you'll need.

.NET Aspire does have some dependencies. If you're already developing with .NET and with containers, you likely already have them. The first and most important is that you need the .NET Software Development Kit (SDK). Generally, if you're reading this book and you're already a .NET developer, you probably already have this. If you don't, the SDK can be installed on Windows, Linux, and Mac and leveraged via the .NET command-line interface. It is also included with installation of Visual

© Dave Rael 2025
D. Rael, *Getting Started with .NET Aspire*, https://doi.org/10.1007/979-8-8688-1521-8_2

Studio (Windows only) or JetBrains Rider (available on Windows, Linux, and Mac). The following sections will include information about making sure you have the SDK and installing it if you don't.

Another dependency for getting the most out of Aspire is a container runtime. Technically, this isn't strictly required. .NET Aspire isn't merely a tool for containers. It's much more than that. Containers are a powerful part of the story and are a great way for software to be packaged, delivered, and leveraged so you'll probably want to use them. Given this, you'll want to have a container runtime installed.

The default for this is Docker, which is most easily installed via Docker Desktop, which runs a Linux virtual machine, the host for your containers. You can find information about installing and getting started with Docker Desktop here: `https://docs.docker.com/get-started/get-docker/`. To use Docker, you need to be aware of its licensing terms and pricing (`https://www.docker.com/pricing`). It does require a paid license for commercial products. Aspire also supports Podman, an open-source alternative to Docker. If you are getting started with containers and don't already know a lot about them, you probably want to use Docker instead of Podman. If you are working on a commercial project and don't want to pay for Docker licensing, it might be worth giving Podman a look.

One way or another, your experience with .NET Aspire will be improved if you have a container runtime on your workstation.

With the .NET SDK and a container runtime in place, you're almost ready to use .NET Aspire, but there's an additional installation step you'll want to make sure you do.

Aspire, itself, does not require a separate installation, but there are solution and project templates you'll want to make sure you have. They are included with installing Visual Studio or Rider, so if you have one of those installed, you probably already have them. If not, you'll want to install the templates.

To make a little clearer what we're getting with the .NET Aspire templates, we'll start with installation from the command line tooling of .NET. After that, we'll look at Visual Studio, Visual Studio Code, and JetBrains Rider.

With the .NET Command-Line Interface

The .NET Aspire project templates are available to install into .NET command-line interface with the .NET SDK.

Following the steps here will require first installing the .NET SDK. Microsoft provides instructions for doing this for whatever platform you're using (https://learn.microsoft.com/dotnet/core/install/).

Visual Studio includes the .NET SDK, so it's already there if you've already installed Visual Studio. If you're not a Visual Studio user and prefer using dotnet, the .NET command-line interface, you can use it to install the templates.

It's worth noting that .NET does ship both runtime and SDK installers. The runtime is needed to execute .NET programs, and the SDK includes the runtime as well as tools for building, packaging, and other operations with .NET code. For the purposes of what we're doing, the runtime is not enough. You need the full SDK.

If you are in a context where you have the .NET SDK installed, but haven't installed the Aspire templates, you'll want to get the templates. To see what the Aspire installation provides, before installing it, try listing the new project templates you have installed matching a query for *aspire*:

```
$ dotnet new list aspire
```

The result should be the very sad message:

```
No templates found matching: 'aspire'
```

Installing the templates can remedy this situation.

```
$ dotnet new install Aspire.ProjectTemplates
```

After executing this installation, trying again to list the new project templates installed bears more fruit:

```
$ dotnet new list aspire
```

results in

```
$ dotnet new list aspire
These templates matched your input: 'aspire'

Template Name                      Short Name               Language
-----------------                  -------------            --------
.NET Aspire App Host               aspire-apphost             [C#]
.NET Aspire Empty App              aspire                     [C#]
.NET Aspire Service Defaults       aspire-servicedefaults     [C#]
.NET Aspire Starter App            aspire-starter             [C#]
.NET Aspire Test Project (MSTest)  aspire-mstest              [C#]
.NET Aspire Test Project (NUnit)   aspire-nunit               [C#]
.NET Aspire Test Project (xUnit)   aspire-xunit               [C#]
```

You have successfully installed the .NET Aspire templates on your workstation.

With Microsoft Visual Studio

The .NET Aspire component comes with Visual Studio. With the default installation, you should already have it. It installs automatically with Visual Studio 2022 version 17.12 or later.

If, in Visual Studio, you invoke the creation of a new project, whether with the assigned keystroke (Ctrl+Shift+N, by default with the default scheme), choosing Create a new project from the start dialog, or via the File menu (File ➤ New Project), you'll see the new project dialog with the ability to filter the new project templates by project type via the dropdown that defaults to saying All project types.

Among the options for project type, you should see .NET Aspire.

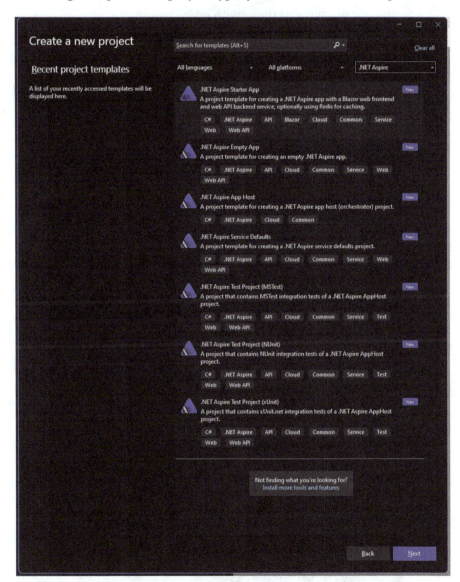

Figure 2-1. *Visual Studio New Project Dialog with .NET Aspire project types selected*

It should not come as a surprise that the templates available for in Visual Studio are the same as those with *dotnet new*.

If you don't see .NET Aspire, you probably don't have the component installed. Open the Visual Studio Installer, click Modify, choose Individual components, and make sure .NET Aspire SDK is selected under the .NET heading. With this installed, you should have the .NET Aspire new project templates.

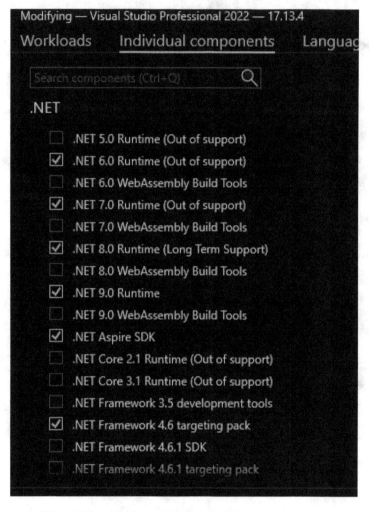

Figure 2-2. *Visual Studio Installer, Individual components tab with .NET Aspire SDK selected*

With JetBrains Rider

The .NET Aspire plugin for JetBrains Rider is bundled with Rider. It is also installed by default, so it's likely you don't need to do anything to install Aspire beyond just installing Rider. If your installation does not include the Aspire plugin, perhaps because of having installed before it was included by default and having not installed it in an update, the plugin can be installed from the *Plugins* tab of the Rider settings dialog.

The following screenshot shows the plugin already installed, but for a Rider instance without the plugin, it can be found and installed in the Plugins part of settings.

Figure 2-3. *JetBrains Rider Plugins settings with search results narrowed to show only the .NET Aspire Rider plugin*

When you choose to create a new solution in Rider, you'll have *Aspire* as an option on the left-side solution type filters in the New Solution dialog.

With *Aspire* selected, the dialog will let you choose which of the templates you want to use via a dropdown list labeled *Type*:

Figure 2-4. *JetBrains Rider New Solution dialog with the Aspire type selected*

The available new solution and project templates available in Rider are a match with those seen via both Visual Studio and the dotnet command-line interface.

With Visual Studio Code

When you write C# code in Visual Studio Code, it will suggest that you should install the C# Dev Kit extension, which provides an experience for C# development with most of the benefits of Visual Studio.

Figure 2-5. *Visual Studio Code C# Dev Kit installed extension information*

In addition to many other language features, it provides support for .NET Aspire and brings the Aspire solution and project templates into Visual Studio Code.

Selecting the right-click menu option for creating a new project in the Solution Explorer provided by the C# Dev Kit will have the Aspire templates as options.

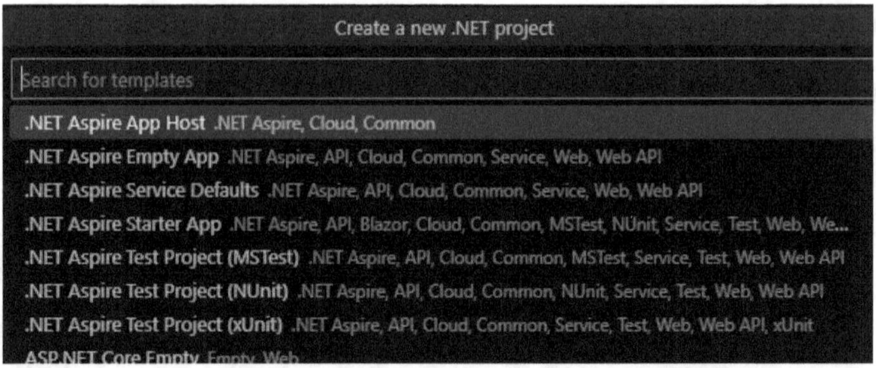

Figure 2-6. *Visual Studio Code .NET: new project command options*

The .NET Aspire templates appear right at the top of the list, even without having to filter (but that's just an accident of starting with a period putting them first in alphabetical order rather than them being prioritized).

Getting to Know the Templates Provided by .NET Aspire

Creating a Sample Project

The best way to get quickly acquainted with .NET Aspire is to start by creating a new solution using the .NET Aspire Starter App. In fact, we'll create more than one project using this template with some different options, inspect what gets generated, and compare what happens differently when we make different choices.

The simplest way we can get started to see what .NET Aspire provides is to use the *Starter App* template without any options.

Before starting with creating projects, I suggest you create a root directory in which to work for the samples we'll create.

Using the .NET command-line interface, from your root directory, create a new project and put it into a directory of its own. That looks like this:

```
$ dotnet new aspire-starter -o Demo.AspireStarter
```

You can do the same thing in Visual Studio, from the *New Project* dialog by selecting *.NET Aspire Starter App* and clicking *Next*. You'll then use the *Configure your new project* step to choose your location, including the name you want to give to your solution (*Demo.AspireStarter* in this example) and click *Next*.

Figure 2-7. *Visual Studio .NET Aspire Starter App solution template dialog flow start*

You'll then just click *Create* again on the *Additional Information* step. It's here that we'll be able to choose some options, but for now, we're just using the defaults.

Figure 2-8. *Visual Studio .NET Aspire Starter App solution template dialog flow further options*

JetBrains Rider also has a similar flow. After choosing to create a new solution, you can select *Starter App* from the *Type* dropdown list.

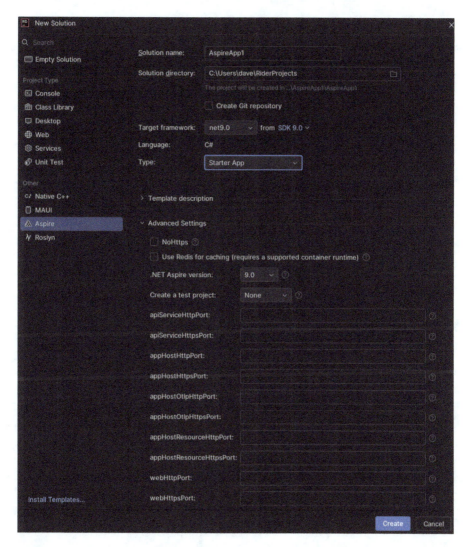

Figure 2-9. JetBrains Rider .NET Aspire Starter App solution template dialog

Your selection of project/solution type will surface the options available for the chosen template in the expandable *Advanced Settings* section of the dialog. The *Create* button will instantiate the template and get you up and running with your new solution.

Via any of these paths, you're now up and running with a .NET Aspire starter project setup.

Note   I wanted to demonstrate with this first part that the dialogs you'll see in the graphical flows of the integrated development environments give you the same options you have using the command-line interface. Going forward, I'll mostly demonstrate using the *dotnet*, rather Visual Studio, Visual Studio Code, or Rider. I'm doing it this way because of a handful of reasons. One is that I simply prefer it. Another is that Visual Studio is only available on Windows, which will not be what all readers are using. It also requires an expensive license for professional use. Rider works on multiple platforms and is less expensive but does still require a paid license (with a temporary trial license available). The command line is the most accessible way of performing these exercises. It's also the most repeatable. You can see exactly the commands I'm issuing rather than trying to follow a narrative of choosing menu options and clicking the right buttons. Know that anything I'm doing with the .NET command-line interface can also be done in integrated development environments and editors.

Digging into What Has Been Created

Let's take a look at what we've made so far. Remember, the only actions we've taken are that we've installed the .NET Aspire templates and we've created a new solution using the *.NET Aspire Starter App* (short name: *aspire-starter*) template.

If we first locate ourselves in the new solution directory, we'll find that it has a .NET solution file and a set of directories containing .NET projects.

Figure 2-10. *New .NET Aspire Starter solution directory structure*

The same thing looks like this in the Visual Studio Solution Explorer.

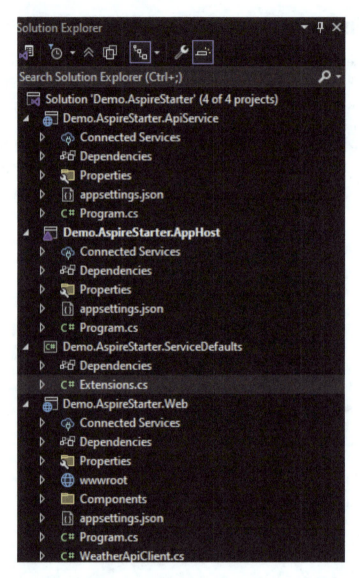

Figure 2-11. *New .NET Aspire Starter solution viewed in the Visual Studio Solution Explorer*

The solution file starts with including each of the project files. This solution will build just like any other .NET solution, complete with restoring packages from nuget.org (by default, or whatever package registry you set up for your project after this initial setup exercise).

The following shows building the solution by using the *dotnet build* command with the .NET SDK installed. The same thing can be done in Visual Studio by using the *Build Solution* command (Ctrl+Shift+B, by default in the default scheme).

```
$ dotnet run --project Demo.AspireStarter.AppHost
Restore complete (5.2s)
  Demo.AspireStarter.ServiceDefaults succeeded (11.0s) →
  Demo.AspireStarter.ServiceDefaults/bin/Debug/net9.0/Demo.
  AspireStarter.ServiceDefaults.dll
  Demo.AspireStarter.ApiService succeeded (4.7s) → Demo.
  AspireStarter.ApiService/bin/Debug/net9.0/Demo.AspireStarter.
  ApiService.dll
  Demo.AspireStarter.Web succeeded (11.3s) → Demo.
  AspireStarter.Web/bin/Debug/net9.0/Demo.AspireStarter.Web.dll
  Demo.AspireStarter.AppHost succeeded (2.6s) → Demo.
  AspireStarter.AppHost/bin/Debug/net9.0/Demo.AspireStarter.
  AppHost.dll

Build succeeded in 32.3s
```

You will have noticed that this template created four projects.

- Demo.AspireStarter.ApiService

- Demo.AspireStarter.AppHost

- Demo.AspireStarter.ServiceDefaults

- Demo.AspireStarter.Web

This setup is a simple distributed system consisting of two main application processes that will host domain functionality reachable via HTTP. Those are the *ApiService* project and the *Web* project. Web is a Blazor frontend web application that depends on the API served by the *ApiService* project. Remember that these projects are just examples of a type of system you might want to create and there are two of them to show what it's like to create a distributed system with .NET Aspire.

These two projects are not terribly different from other projects you've likely seen before in the case of creating application code with .NET, ASP.NET Core, Blazor, and such technologies. They do differ slightly in that they reference packages specific to .NET Aspire that help with service location, observability, orchestration, and other concerns of distributed systems. There will be more to say about that in a moment.

The other two projects are particularly interesting to consider as you become familiar with .NET Aspire.

The a*pp host* project is the starting point for being able to run your distributed system. In fact, it is the center of the magic of .NET Aspire. To run the whole system, all you need to do is run the app host project.

From the command line, that looks like

```
$ dotnet run --project Demo.AspireStarter.AppHost
```

Or you can notice in Visual Studio in the solution properties that the default setup is to have the app host project as the startup project for when you run from Visual Studio (with or without debugging).

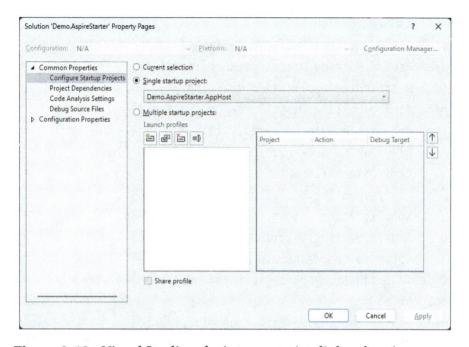

Figure 2-12. *Visual Studio solution properties dialog showing AppHost as single startup project*

In prior experiences with solutions with multiple executable projects, you might have configured Visual Studio to launch multiple startup projects or scripted bringing up multiple processes. These measures are not necessary with .NET Aspire. By simply running the app host project, the system starts up, including a dashboard visible in your browser.

Before looking at any of the code and packages included in the projects generated from instantiating the template, let's just try running our app host project. The output of *dotnet run* looks like this:

```
Using launch settings from
Demo.AspireStarter.AppHost/Properties/launchSettings.json...
Building...
info: Aspire.Hosting.DistributedApplication[0]
```

```
        Aspire version:
        9.1.0+2a8f48ea5811f317a26405eb315aa315cc9e3cea
info: Aspire.Hosting.DistributedApplication[0]
        Distributed application starting.
info: Aspire.Hosting.DistributedApplication[0]
        Application host directory is: /home/raelyard/code/
        play/aspire-book-code/Demo.AspireStarter/Demo.
        AspireStarter.AppHost
info: Aspire.Hosting.DistributedApplication[0]
        Now listening on: https://localhost:17086
info: Aspire.Hosting.DistributedApplication[0]
        Login to the dashboard at
https://localhost:17086/login?t=7a40edc94e0ac9097a3ae
2d625ebbfb4
info: Aspire.Hosting.DistributedApplication[0]
        Distributed application started. Press Ctrl+C to
        shut down.
```

Note that this output gives a locally accessible address on which we can request a dashboard for the distributed system when it says "Now listening on: https://localhost:17240" (note that your port will likely be different) and it gives a token allowing access to the dashboard with this message (note that your port your token will be different): "Login to the dashboard at https://localhost:17086/login?t=7a40edc94e0ac9097a3ae 2d625ebbfb4".

Loading this in the browser, we see something like the following:

Figure 2-13. *.NET Aspire dashboard for solution created from the aspire-starter template*

There are a few things to notice here. One is that this page shows that our distributed system shows two resources. Both are running and they are our .NET projects. You can see in the rightmost column that both resources are of type *Project*. We'll see other types of resources shortly as we exercise some other options of the start template to set up some other system elements. Notice also that both project resources have a name, and they are both in the state *Running*. There are also links on the dashboard to view both logs and details for each of these resources.

Clicking the logs link shows you exactly what you expect: logs for the running process.

Figure 2-14. *Viewing console logs in the .NET Aspire dashboard*

Clicking on details gives a drilled-in look at runtime information for a given resource.

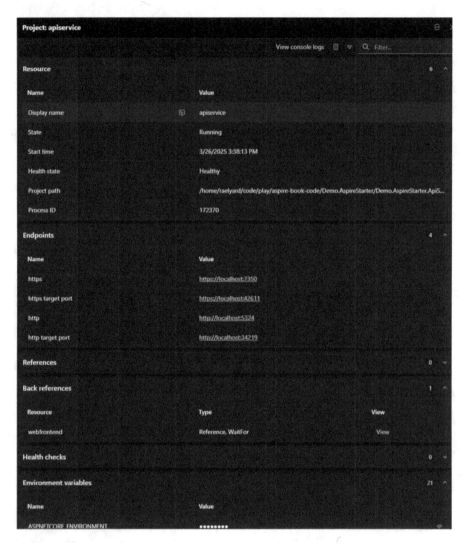

Figure 2-15. *Resource details in the .NET Aspire dashboard*

Among the details presented for a running project are the values seen in the Resources table as well as the set of environment variables available to the running process. By default, the environment variables are hidden, but they can be easily exposed with button clicks in the browser user interface, making troubleshooting easier than it would otherwise be.

In the App Host Project

It is particularly interesting to look at how the app host project is laid out in the *Program.cs* main entry point file. Having used the aspire-starter template with no options, the *Program.cs* looks like this:

```
var builder = DistributedApplication.CreateBuilder(args);

var apiService = builder.AddProject<Projects. Demo.
AspireStarter _ApiService>("apiservice");

builder.AddProject<Projects. Demo.AspireStarter _Web>("webfrontend")
    .WithExternalHttpEndpoints()
    .WithReference(apiService);

builder.Build().Run();
```

Notice that there's an application builder instance present, much like the *WebApplicationBuilder* or *ApplicationBuilder* classes you might use in an ASP.NET Core application. .NET Aspire provides the *IDistributedApplicationBuilder* interface for the purpose of creating a host for your distributed system. It's elegant and smooth that the process is so similar to what you are already familiar with if you're experienced with using the .NET Generic Host (you can find documentation here: https://learn. microsoft.com/dotnet/core/extensions/generic-host). Calling the *CreateBuilder()* static factory method on the *DistributedApplication* class yields an instance of the *IDistributedApplicationBuilder* interface, with which you can register dependencies for running your distributed application. The template we've instantiated gives a simple, useful example of doing just that.

This setup creates the builder and then registers the *ApiService* project with it. It follows that by adding the Web project and gives it a dependency on the ApiService project. This sets up an order of setup and that one project will require the other. This will also enable service discovery so that the Web project is able to locate the ApiService project. I'll say more about that later.

Finally, the *Build* method is called on the builder to return the *DistrubutedApplication* instance, which is started up by calling *Run()*.

Both of these elements of the broader distributed application are added to the distributed application host by calling *AddProject()*. That's because both of these dependencies for the system are .NET projects.

In moments, we'll see other types of resources that can be included, but first, there's more to see about what's happening to create the magic of the running resources and the dashboard we've already encountered.

The *Program.cs* file isn't the only interesting file generated by the template in the app host project. Let's next look at the project file. Using the example output name from before, that file, in the *Demo.AspireStarter. AppHost* directory, is called *Demo.AspireStarter.csproj*. It looks like this:

```
<Project Sdk="Microsoft.NET.Sdk">

  <Sdk Name="Aspire.AppHost.Sdk" Version="9.1.0" />

  <PropertyGroup>
    <OutputType>Exe</OutputType>
    <TargetFramework>net9.0</TargetFramework>
    <ImplicitUsings>enable</ImplicitUsings>
    <Nullable>enable</Nullable>
    <IsAspireHost>true</IsAspireHost>
    <UserSecretsId>fda5787c-5157-4fe8-a769-80e753fd2390
    </UserSecretsId>
  </PropertyGroup>

  <ItemGroup>
    <ProjectReference Include="..\Demo.AspireStarter.
    ApiService\Demo.AspireStarter.ApiService.csproj" />
    <ProjectReference Include="..\Demo.AspireStarter.Web\Demo.
    AspireStarter.Web.csproj" />
  </ItemGroup>
```

```
<ItemGroup>
  <PackageReference Include="Aspire.Hosting.AppHost"
  Version="9.1.0" />
</ItemGroup>
</Project>
```

The things to notice in this file are that there are references to the two executable http endpoint projects and a package reference to *Aspire.Hosting.AppHost*. It's via this NuGet package, published by the .NET Aspire team, that we're able to create the *DistributedApplication* host and set up the various resources that make up our distributed application.

In the ServiceDefaults Project

The project file in the project called *Demo.AspireStarter.ServiceDefaults* is filled with a greater number of package references. The content of *Demo.AspireStarter.ServiceDefaults.csproj* looks like this:

```
<Project Sdk="Microsoft.NET.Sdk">

  <PropertyGroup>
    <TargetFramework>net9.0</TargetFramework>
    <ImplicitUsings>enable</ImplicitUsings>
    <Nullable>enable</Nullable>
    <IsAspireSharedProject>true</IsAspireSharedProject>
  </PropertyGroup>

  <ItemGroup>
    <FrameworkReference Include="Microsoft.AspNetCore.App" />

    <PackageReference Include="Microsoft.Extensions.Http.
    Resilience" Version="9.2.0" />
```

```
<PackageReference Include="Microsoft.Extensions.
ServiceDiscovery" Version="9.1.0" />
<PackageReference Include="OpenTelemetry.Exporter.
OpenTelemetryProtocol" Version="1.9.0" />
<PackageReference Include="OpenTelemetry.Extensions.
Hosting" Version="1.9.0" />
<PackageReference Include="OpenTelemetry.Instrumentation.
AspNetCore" Version="1.9.0" />
<PackageReference Include="OpenTelemetry.Instrumentation.
Http" Version="1.9.0" />
<PackageReference Include="OpenTelemetry.Instrumentation.
Runtime" Version="1.9.0" />
  </ItemGroup>

</Project>
```

First notice that this project does not have any references to any of the other projects created with this template and that it does reference several NuGet packages. Notice, also, that the packages referenced do not include *Aspire* anywhere in their names.

These packages are included to set up some core needs for the pieces of the distributed application. These needs include the likes of telemetry, health checks, and service discovery. Telemetry is included that conforms to a popular open-source framework called OpenTelemetry, which is why many of the packages include that name.

The main thrust of what is provided by the ServiceDefaults project is shared in the way of exposing extension methods that can be used in the individual process projects in the distributed application.

The following shows the method signatures (without the bodies, for brevity, just to show the signatures) of the methods in the *Extensions.cs* static class in the ServiceDefaults project.

```
public static class Extensions
{
    public static IHostApplicationBuilder
    AddServiceDefaults(this IHostApplicationBuilder builder);
    public static IHostApplicationBuilder
    ConfigureOpenTelemetry(this IHostApplicationBuilder
    builder);
    private static IHostApplicationBuilder
    AddOpenTelemetryExporters(this IHostApplicationBuilder
    builder);
    public static IHostApplicationBuilder
    AddDefaultHealthChecks(this IHostApplicationBuilder
    builder);
    public static WebApplication MapDefaultEndpoints(this
    WebApplication app);
}
```

Notice that these are all extension methods that operate either on an *IHostApplicationBuilder* or on an already built *WebApplication*. The utility of these methods will become clearer as we notice how they are used in the *Web* and *ApiService* projects, both of which reference the *ServiceDefaults* project to make use of the extension methods provided. Notice, also, that the app host project doesn't need to reference the service defaults project. It's building a *DistributedApplication* rather than a *WebApplication* and doesn't make use of the services provided.

The *Extensions* class generated from the starter template provides a set of useful extensions with the ability to customize, extend, and add to them for the needs of your distributed application.

In the Application Endpoint Projects

Let's now turn our attention to the remaining projects in this solution. These are the directories called *Demo.AspireStarter.ApiService* and *Demo. AspireStarter.Web*

These are similar enough to talk about them together. In fact, the content of their project files is identical. Both *Demo.AspireStarter. ApiService.csproj* and *Demo.AspireStarter.Web.csproj* read as follows.

```
<Project Sdk="Microsoft.NET.Sdk.Web">

  <PropertyGroup>
    <TargetFramework>net9.0</TargetFramework>
    <ImplicitUsings>enable</ImplicitUsings>
    <Nullable>enable</Nullable>
  </PropertyGroup>

  <ItemGroup>
    <ProjectReference Include="..\Demo.AspireStarter.Service
    Defaults\Demo.AspireStarter.ServiceDefaults.csproj" />
  </ItemGroup>

  <ItemGroup>
    <PackageReference Include="Microsoft.AspNetCore.OpenApi"
    Version="9.0.2" />
  </ItemGroup>

</Project>
```

The interesting thing here is that, as mentioned in the above section related to the service defaults projects, both reference that project directly.

The *Program.cs* class files in these projects differ from one another, but both make use of extension methods provided by *ServiceDefaults*. They have calls to *builder.AddServiceDefaults()* and *app.MapDefaultEndpoints()* in common. These are both extension methods from the *Extensions* class.

The former is for registering services for telemetry, service discovery, health checks, and such, and the latter is for setting up paths in the applications that, when requested, will respond with the health checks as set up in the *ServiceDefaults* project. This gives a single place to customize how you want your health checks to work and how to request them in a way that is standard across your solution.

Also notice the code in the *Web* project's *Program.cs* that sets up *HttpClient* to communicate with the running *ApiService* project with the following line:

```
builder.Services.AddHttpClient<WeatherApiClient>(client =>
    {
        // This URL uses "https+http://" to indicate HTTPS is
            preferred over HTTP.
        // Learn more about service discovery scheme resolution
            at https://aka.ms/dotnet/sdschemes.
        client.BaseAddress = new("https+http://apiservice");
    });
```

This capability is coming from the *Microsoft.Extensions. ServiceDiscovery* package, which is not specific to Aspire, but is used by Aspire and one of the packages referenced by the service defaults project.

In this call to *AddHttpClient*, a registration is set up with the service registry such that a base address reference with the name *apiservice* is added as a dependency for the *Web* application. Because of the call in the app host project we saw earlier to register the *Web* project with a dependency on the *ApiService* project with the name *apiservice* (notice that this name matches the registration of the base address for the *HttpClient*), the service discovery resolution is hooked up. The *Microsoft. Extensions.ServiceDiscovery* uses a default configuration-based resolver that gets the address needed from configuration with a convention based on the name. As such, when the *app host* starts and it, in turn, starts the *ApiService* and the *Web* projects, it injects an environment variable into the

process space for *Web*. Because of this, Web can resolve the right address
for the API on which it depends at runtime when running via the app host.

This eases the burden of needing to create extensive configuration for
running on a workstation environment and makes it quick and easy to get
up and running with a working environment without an excess of fuss.

You can see this in action by running the *app host*, viewing the
dashboard in your browser, selecting the *webfrontend* project resource,
clicking on the eye image to view environment variable values, and
scrolling all the way to the bottom of the shown environment variables.

Figure 2-16. *.NET Aspire service discovery visualized as environment
variables in the .NET Aspire dashboard*

You should see values injected for *services__apiservice__http__0* and
services__apiservice__https__0 that have values for localhost addresses
with ports on which your *ApiService* is running. These can be checked
against what you see in the *apiservice* resource, and you should find that
they are consistent.

Note   The names of these values might look a little odd if you're
not familiar with the .NET configuration system and how it works
with various sources of configuration. Configuration can be set up
in JSON files with a hierarchical structure, and they can also exist
in other places, like vaults, user secrets, environment variables,
and more. When using a store without a hierarchical nature, the
standard configuration will use a colon (:) as a hierarchy separator
such that an environment variable named *services:apiservice:http:0*
would match to a JSON hierarchy with those elements nested within

one another. Using colons works fine with environment variables on Windows, but not on other platforms, so an alternate form is supported as well. Instead of colons, two underscore characters (__) can be used as the hierarchy level separator. This is why these environment variables provided to the *Web* project by the app host look like they do. *services__apiservice__https__0* is equivalent to *services:apiservice:https:0* and works across multiple platforms more consistently.

This is .NET Aspire service discovery in action, and if you visit the web application, you'll see that it gets randomly selected values for dummy weather forecast from the API successfully.

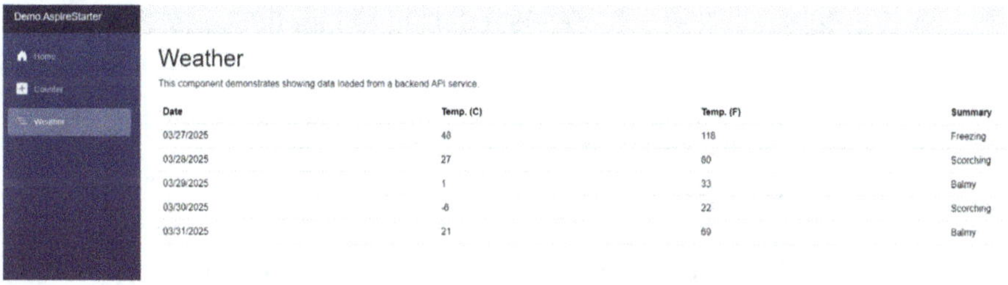

Figure 2-17. *Viewing the webfrontend project in the browser, running via the app host in a solution created with the aspire-starter solution template*

These projects are simple but give an idea of what is possible with .NET Aspire.

What we've done so far is use a template to create a starter project with a *ServiceDefaults* project, an *app host*, an API, and a web frontend. We only had to run a single project to get the whole system working, including a handy dashboard with links to the running application processes, logs, metrics, and a summary of the runtime environment resources.

We've gotten quite a lot without having to do a whole lot. There's still more to see, though.

The Starter Template with an Integration

Our first instantiation of the *aspire-starter* template didn't specify any options, though I did mention it offers some optional parameters. To see a little more of what Aspire can do, let's create another solution using the same template, but this time with an option to enable using Redis for ASP. NET output caching.

With Visual Studio, this amounts to checking a checkbox that was shown in the screenshots earlier. With the dotnet command-line interface, it's specified in the call to create the new solution.

Note   If you're still in the solution directory we created earlier for the Demo.AspireStarter solution, you'll want to back out one directory higher to create our new solution as a sibling to that directory with *cd* ...

```
$ dotnet new aspire-starter --use-redis-cache -o Demo.
AspireStarterWithRedis
```

The new solution directory structure will look identical (except for having given everything a slightly different name) to the prior one at the top level with the same directories and files created.

Figure 2-18. *New .NET Aspire Starter solution with Redis cache directory structure*

There are some differences in the content of the generated files and in the resulting output. Viewing these differences will start with running the *app host* project and seeing what we see in the resulting dashboard in the browser.

```
$ dotnet run --project Demo.AspireStarterWithRedis.AppHost run
```

Figure 2-19. *.NET Aspire dashboard for solution created from the aspire-starter template with Redis cache, showing the Redis instance as a container resource*

Note   For this to work, you need to have a container runtime installed and running on your machine. This is easiest to accomplish with Docker Desktop.

The dashboard looks the same as the starter without having exercised the Redis option except that there's now a third resource that wasn't there in the other solution. It shouldn't come as a surprise that the name of this resource is *cache*. It might not be expected to see that it has a different type from the other resources. The *apiservice* and *webfrontend* resources are of type *Project*, and this new *cache* resource is of type *Container*.

This container resource was created by leveraging the Docker runtime on your workstation to create a container from an image in a container registry, specifically, in this case, from the image *docker.io/library/redis:7.4*.

This shows that .NET Aspire is able not only to leverage project code you write in .NET, but also container workloads.

This is our first look at a .NET Aspire *integration*. There will be more to say about integrations in Chapter 6. For now, we can see that we have a new resource and will look at what has changed in the source between the two solutions that enabled the inclusion of the container resource.

In the AppHost Project

Looking first in the AppHost project, the project file looks like this:

```
<Project Sdk="Microsoft.NET.Sdk">

  <Sdk Name="Aspire.AppHost.Sdk" Version="9.1.0" />

  <PropertyGroup>
    <OutputType>Exe</OutputType>
    <TargetFramework>net9.0</TargetFramework>
    <ImplicitUsings>enable</ImplicitUsings>
    <Nullable>enable</Nullable>
    <IsAspireHost>true</IsAspireHost>
    <UserSecretsId>6cf378fe-bae5-49d2-bed3-b6bfc381905d
    </UserSecretsId>
  </PropertyGroup>
```

```xml
<ItemGroup>
  <ProjectReference Include="..\Demo.AspireStarterWithRedis.
  ApiService\Demo.AspireStarterWithRedis.ApiService.
  csproj" />
  <ProjectReference Include="..\Demo.AspireStarterWithRedis.
  Web\Demo.AspireStarterWithRedis.Web.csproj" />
</ItemGroup>
<ItemGroup>
  <PackageReference Include="Aspire.Hosting.AppHost"
  Version="9.1.0" />
  <PackageReference Include="Aspire.Hosting.Redis"
  Version="9.1.0" />
</ItemGroup>
</Project>
```

This is the same as the other app host project file except for one difference. The lone addition here is a package reference to *Aspire.Hosting. Redis*. It becomes evident that Aspire integrations are added via references to NuGet packages specific to a given integration.

Program.cs is also largely the same, with only small additions.

```csharp
var builder = DistributedApplication.CreateBuilder(args);

var cache = builder.AddRedis("cache");

var apiService = builder.AddProject<Projects. Demo.
AspireStarterWithRedis_ApiService>("apiservice");

builder.AddProject<Projects. Demo.AspireStarterWithRedis _
Web>("webfrontend")
    .WithExternalHttpEndpoints()
    .WithReference(cache)
    .WithReference(apiService);

builder.Build().Run();
```

There's a new line included, adding a *cache* resource via a call to *builder.AddRedis("cache")*.

The inclusion of the *Web* project in the distributed application in the prior solution only included the addition of a reference to *apiService*. It now also includes adding a reference to the *cache* resource.

```
builder.AddProject<Projects. Demo.AspireStarterWithRedis _Web>
("webfrontend")
    .WithExternalHttpEndpoints()
    .WithReference(cache)
    .WithReference(apiService);
```

This sets up a dependency similar to that of the *Web* project to the *ApiService* project. Now, the web project is injected with configuration enabling service discovery for both the API and the Redis instance running in a container via the Docker engine on the workstation.

In the Web Project

Updating to use the Redis cache in the *aspire-starter* template does not change anything in the *ApiService* project. One certainly could design an API using a cache via a key-value store like Redis, but this template doesn't do that. If it did, we'd have seen the app host project adding a dependency on the cache to the ApiService project. Instead, the template, with the *--use-redis-cache* option, only makes use of the caching via Redis in the *Web* project. Specifically, it's using ASP.NET Core output caching with Redis as the backing store.

We can see this in the *Web* project file with a reference to the *Aspire.StackExchange.Redis.OutputCaching* NuGet package.

```
<Project Sdk="Microsoft.NET.Sdk.Web">

  <PropertyGroup>
    <TargetFramework>net9.0</TargetFramework>
```

```
  <ImplicitUsings>enable</ImplicitUsings>
  <Nullable>enable</Nullable>
</PropertyGroup>

<ItemGroup>
  <ProjectReference Include="..\Demo.AspireStarterWithRedis.
  ServiceDefaults\Demo.AspireStarterWithRedis.
  ServiceDefaults.csproj" />
</ItemGroup>

<ItemGroup>
  <PackageReference Include="Aspire.StackExchange.Redis.
  OutputCaching" Version="9.1.0" />

</ItemGroup>

</Project>
```

This package, specifically, makes use of a Redis data store for ASP.NET Core output caching, meaning that when ASP.NET generates an output payload for a page it serves, it will hold that output in a cache to serve future requests without having to generate it again.

The *Program.cs* process start class makes use of this package by calling the *builder.AddRedisOutputCache("cache")* extension method from this package. Similar to the reference to the *apiservice* name we saw earlier, this leverages a default configuration provider for service location that makes use of configuration via environment variable injected into the process space by the app host.

Given this setup of service location, the *Web* process is able to connect to both the *ApiService* process and the Redis container and it just works.

The Aspire dashboard will show the environment variable in question for the connection string for the Redis cache as the value *ConnectionStrings__cache*, similar to how it does for the API.

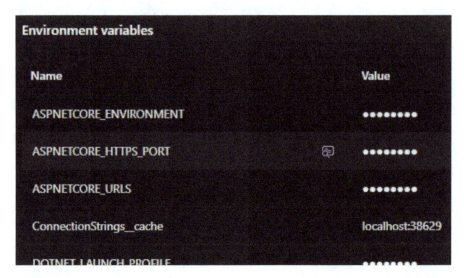

Figure 2-20. *.NET Aspire dashboard showing environment variable for webfrontend resource for connection string for reaching cache resource, according to .NET Aspire service discovery*

Building Your Own Solution from Scratch

Now that we've looked at the starter template provided by .NET Aspire to get an idea of what it looks like to use Aspire, let's walk down the path of starting fresh.

As a general rule, when starting a new software project, the first thing you'll want to do is create a project for unit tests to start to flesh out what you want to do in the domain of the problem you're tackling. Even though this book is not about unit testing, we'll go ahead and do that because it's a good way to proceed. So, I'll start by creating a new directory and taking some starting actions for having a solution with a test project. My preference for unit testing is xUnit, so I'll use it for my testing project.

Note   .NET Aspire does have a test project template and we'll cover what that is for in Chapter 5, but it's geared toward running your distributed system within a testing context and is, therefore, an integration testing toolset. As such, we'll not use that for creating a unit test project.

The actions taken here can be done in Visual Studio, Visual Studio Code, or Rider in addition to using the dotnet command-line interface. I'll show this with *dotnet* both to offer some exposure to ways of doing things many .NET developers don't necessarily do normally and because it's repeatable for you to follow along. These commands are almost all dotnet commands and will therefore work from any shell on any platform supported by dotnet. For commands like creating directories, I'll be using POSIX-shell compatible commands because I'm working in zsh on Linux, and PowerShell has aliases for these commands such that they'll also work in PowerShell. For the cmd shell on Windows, you'd use *md* instead of *mkdir*.

First, create a directory for the solution and change your terminal context into the new directory.

```
$ mkdir Demo.AspireNew
$ cd Demo.AspireNew
```

You're now ready to start your .NET solution with a solution file to serve as an entry point for loading the whole solution in Visual Studio and a target for building from the command line.

```
$ dotnet new sln
```

49

To start with a project for unit testing, you can use any of the new project templates provided for this purpose. My preference is to use xUnit. That looks like this.

```
$ dotnet new xunit -o Test
```

To have a useful solution, we'll want to add any new projects to the solution so they're included in build commands and in using Visual Studio.

```
$ dotnet sln add Test
```

So far, none of this has had anything to do with .NET Aspire. If I were really starting a project in this way, I'd have already initialized a Git repository, added a Readme file with some documentation of what I intend to do and began with writing some tests to assert what I want a function to do and build out my logic that way, with application code right in the test project that I'd move into an ultimate home where I come to a need for having a process to run.

For our purposes here, I'll skip ahead to having decided that now I need to create a distributed system with multiple pieces.

As such, we'll want to create the elements of an Aspire system. That will involve creating, minimally, a ServiceDefaults project and an app host project. Let's do just that.

Start with creating a service defaults project and adding it to the solution.

```
$ dotnet new aspire-servicedefaults -o ServiceDefaults
$ dotnet sln add ServiceDefaults
```

Also create an app host project and add it to the solution.

```
$ dotnet new aspire-apphost -o AppHost
$ dotnet sln add AppHost
```

Now, we have the root projects one needs for running a distributed system. That's good and you could, at this point, use *dotnet run --project AppHost* and see the dashboard run. You could do that, but it would be boring because we're not actually creating any resources yet – we don't yet have any projects or integrations for the processes that will make up our distributed system. Let's fix that by first creating an API project and enlisting it in our app host distributed application setup.

We could start by adding integrations, but it's more fundamental that we're able to create .NET process projects to run our own code. If we don't do that, there's really not much reason to use .NET Aspire or even .NET at all. We'll get to integrations in Chapter 6, but for now, we'll create an API we can run as a part of a system.

```
$ dotnet new webapi -o Api
$ dotnet sln add Api
```

This creates a sample API project, but doesn't yet enlist it in our distributed application. To do that, we're going to have to make our app host aware of this project by first adding a reference to it, then including it in the distributed application startup code.

```
$ dotnet add AppHost reference Api
```

The code in the *Program.cs* in the *app host* project here is noticeably simpler than that of the starter template we created earlier. Straight from the app host template, it just looks like

```
var builder = DistributedApplication.CreateBuilder(args);
builder.Build().Run();
```

We'll want to expand this code to include our *Api* project.

```
var builder = DistributedApplication.CreateBuilder(args);
builder.AddProject<Projects.Api>("api");
builder.Build().Run();
```

This is enough to enlist our *Api* project in the distributed application, but it's not yet complete because we want to include our ServiceDefaults so that we have all of the health monitoring and standard telemetry we expect from our applications. This means adding a reference in *Api* to the *ServiceDefaults* project and calling the *AddServiceDefaults()* extension method in the process startup code.

```
dotnet add Api reference ServiceDefaults
```

Then in *Program.cs* in the Api project directory, we'll want to add a call to *builder.AddServiceDefaults()* right after the first line creating the builder.

Now, running the app host project will yield a dashboard showing a resource.

Figure 2-21. *.NET Aspire dashboard for a slim app model with only a single Api project*

The "distributed system" we've set up at this point is not something worthy of that name. It includes only a single process, but it does illustrate the way you can create a solution, a unit test project, .NET Aspire projects for enabling straightforward distributed systems work and adding a project resource to your distributed system. These are the building blocks for using .NET Aspire to create a systems-building experience that will work for your team in a productive manner.

I could continue here by adding more pieces to this solution, but I think this is adequate for the purposes of seeing how a solution is structured that makes use of .NET Aspire and understanding what the templates provide. You can continue from here to add other project resources and see what happens when you include them in the app model by adding them in the Program.cs file in the app host project.

Summary

This chapter started with getting set up by installing the necessary dependencies and tools for using .NET Aspire. We then looked at the solution and project templates available for Aspire systems and how they appear in a handful of development environments.

From there, we just used the templates to try creating sample solutions and seeing them run. We capitalized on the opportunity to study the templates and what they created and to examine and run the code to get an idea of what .NET Aspire really does. We got a little experience with seeing the types of projects we'll have in a solution using .NET Aspire and what distinguishes them.

We got a glimpse at a .NET Aspire integration and witnessed a workload running in a container to serve our system. We also saw the dashboard provided by Aspire in action.

We got started with .NET Aspire. There's still a lot more to learn. In the next chapter, we'll review the types of projects with a little more rigor. We'll discuss the templates, resources, and projects we saw in the exercises in this chapter and try to understand their intent.

CHAPTER 3

.NET Aspire Project Types and Templates

Having looked at the starter solution template supplied by .NET Aspire in the prior chapter as a starting point for getting familiar with the structure and projects in a .NET Aspire solution, let's look more closely at the types of projects and other resources you'll want to include in solutions for building distributed systems. We saw some of what goes into these projects when looking at the output of creating from the template called aspire-sample, but we'll dive a little further into what they are, what they have, and the purposes they serve, as well as introducing Aspire-specific support for running integration tests against your running distributed system.

In addition to looking closer at the project types, I'll make certain you have familiarity with the solution and project templates available with .NET Aspire. Also, there are a few more things to say about the Aspire dashboard I'll include in this chapter.

You probably already have a pretty good idea of the content and intent of these project types already, but this will reinforce those impressions and discuss what they offer more abstractly. You also had a look at the project and solution templates included with .NET Aspire, but there's a bit more to say about those as well.

© Dave Rael 2025
D. Rael, *Getting Started with .NET Aspire*, https://doi.org/10.1007/979-8-8688-1521-8_3

Projects in a Solution with .NET Aspire

A fundamental building block of a .NET solution is a project, so it's worth looking closely at the projects you'll see.

The App Host Project

By now you should have a reasonable idea of the intent of the app host project. It's an orchestrator for composing the many pieces of a distributed system into a cohesive whole that solves a real software problem.

We looked at the project (.csproj) file generated for app host projects from Aspire templates as well as the *Program.cs* class that runs the system and noted how it uses an *IDistributedApplicationBuilder* instance to set up the system components and the way they relate to one another.

You may have noticed that when you reference a .NET project from your AppHost project, some code is generated to enable treating that project as a type from your system startup code. It's because of this code generation via the .NET Aspire SDK that we're able to, from the main entry point of the distributed system in the *Program.cs* make calls to *IDistributedApplicationBuilder.AddProject<T>()* with generic parameters leveraging types in the *Projects* namespace.

The *Projects* namespace is not an ordinary .NET namespace, and project references in an app host project are not ordinary project references. Rather, when you add a reference to a project in an app host project, the Aspire SDK triggers a generator to create a class implementing an interface called IProjectMetadata (from the *Aspire.Hosting namespace*). The inclusion of the SDK in the project file via the element that looks like *<Sdk Name="Aspire.AppHost.Sdk" Version="9.1.0" />* (note that the version here was the latest at the time of writing, but is likely not at a later time) is what makes this happen via MSBuild. This generated class represents your project that runs as an independent process and can enlist it in the model built by the AppHost project.

This model, built up by the *IDistributedApplicationBuilder*, is called the "application model" or "app model." When you design a distributed system with .NET Aspire, you set it up via the setup of the app model.

Your *Program.cs* file in your app host project is essentially an articulation of your app model. In other words, you design a model for a distributed system, leveraging project metadata and *integrations* to define the elements of your system and the ways they relate to one another. Further, you can do all of this in the same language you are using to build your system projects (if you are using .NET for some/all of your system projects). For most .NET developers, this is C#, but it could be any supported .NET language.

Orchestration of system components via the app host project certainly supports using .NET for the process projects making up the custom software of your system, but other languages and platforms are supported as well. Chances are, if you're interested in .NET Aspire, you probably intend to use .NET for at least some of your system, but perhaps not all of it. Even with .NET technology like Blazor making waves and gaining mindshare and market share for user interface, client-side user interface application JavaScript toolsets like React, Vue, and more have a place in a great many system designs.

.NET Aspire orchestration supports multiple languages, including native .NET languages, JavaScript via Node or npm, and Python. Further, if you have any other type of process code you want to include in your system, you can include it as a container by either referencing it from a registry or via the inclusion of building from a Dockerfile. There are also community-driven *integrations* available for hosting other types of software components using other languages, like Go and Java. One way or another, you should be able to enlist your system components in the orchestrator known as the .NET Aspire app host.

Integrations can also be referenced from the AppHost project for inclusion in the broader system. Integrations are NuGet packages providing seamless addition of cloud-native components into Aspire systems. There are official integrations published by .NET Aspire as well as "Community Toolkit" integrations not supported by the .NET Aspire team, but publicly available and supported by the open-source community. The documentation for integrations at https://learn.microsoft.com/ dotnet/aspire/fundamentals/integrations-overview has a wealth of information about integrations broadly as well as lists of official integrations (broken down into lists that are cloud-agnostic, specific to Azure, and specific to Amazon Web Services (AWS)) and community toolkit integrations. It's a great resource for finding integrations useful for your situation. In addition to these integrations already available, custom integrations are also possible so you can build your own if you have a need.

I'll cover integrations and provide some samples of using them in Chapter 6, but they're worth mentioning here in the context of resources that are orchestrated by the AppHost. The Redis cache resource included in Chapter 2 when using the .NET Aspire starter solution template with the *–use-redis-cache* option is an example of an integration.

The Service Defaults Project

The service defaults project is a great place to set up a common set of cross-cutting concerns for the many projects in your .NET Aspire distributed system. The application endpoint processes, with simple calls to the extension methods from the Service Defaults process, can make use of what you have set up as the defaults for service discovery, telemetry, health checks, and more.

Typically, you'll just call *builder.AddServiceDefaults()* to get a majority of this goodness using the *WebApplicationBuilder* (or another form of host builder) in the *Program.cs* file in your application process project. You'll also call *app.MapDefaultEndpoints*() to register health checks and liveness checks to well-known and expected default paths where they can be requested to monitor the running process. The defaults generated by the template are not necessarily going to be the defaults you want to use, and you'll be able to make your services defaults do what you prefer.

A new service defaults project, created from the *dotnet new* templates provided by .NET Aspire, contains a set of defaults that are useful. You've already seen that when we used the starter template to create a solution, the projects it created had service discovery and telemetry hooked up in a way that just worked right out of the box. You are then at liberty to customize the defaults to suit the needs of your system.

The *Extensions.cs* static class in the service defaults project surfaces the AddServiceDefaults extension method, as well as several other functions it calls to create a one-stop shop for setting up common needs and a single point to customize.

The main functionalities the service defaults project sets up via extension methods are telemetry, health checks, and service discovery. Using the default *Extensions.cs* class generated by either the *aspire-servicedefaults* project template or the *aspire-starter* solution template, you start with sane defaults for setting up these important concerns.

The defaults for telemetry send metrics, traces, and structured logs to an OpenTelemetry endpoint. The default is to send the telemetry to the Aspire dashboard, which can receive and display the information. Sending this information to a collector that makes sense for a deployed environment is something that can be configured without having to change code or it can be customized with code. Chapter 8 will cover observability, which includes and builds on the telemetry collected via this setup.

.NET Aspire defaults for health checks include the registration of ASP. NET Core health checks and the mapping of the default http endpoints in the development environment. These default endpoints are at the paths /*health* and /*alive*. Requests to these paths will surface health responses. They are disabled by default for nondevelopment environments because they can pose a risk for attacks on websites, like denial-of-service. They can be enabled with customization to enable use by orchestrators like Kubernetes or monitoring systems, but care should be taken to protect against abuse and attacks. These protections can include only surfacing these paths on a private network or using IP address restrictions for serving them. There are a host of other ways to customize health checks in a standardized way across your system in addition to adding individual health checks to different applications in the system.

We saw a little of what service discovery does in .NET Aspire with running projects created from the starter template and seeing the environment variables hooked into the runtime environment of the application processes that feed the service discovery mechanism.

The Integration Test Project

Among the project templates included with .NET Aspire for *dotnet new* or new projects in Visual Studio, there are three for creating a test project. These are *aspire-mstest*, *aspire-nunit*, and *aspire-xunit*. They differ only in which testing framework they use for defining tests and assertions, not in how they operate with respect to your .NET Aspire distributed system.

The test project templates included with .NET Aspire are intended more toward integration testing than unit testing. A proper treatment of the different ways of testing and why and when you want to use one vs. another is worthy of treatment in a book all to itself. For our purposes here, it's worth saying that you'll want to do testing both scoped to individual "units" of functionality (unit testing) with tests that execute single functions or small set of code without any dependencies on system components, data stores, or anything external to simply application logic and broader tests that run tests against executing system and application processes and with, potentially, a set of running dependencies. This latter type of testing is often called system testing, integration testing, or, if the scope is sufficiently large, end-to-end testing. There are many differing opinions on where the boundaries lie between tests that fall into these differing categories, but the important distinction in the context of .NET Aspire test projects is that of testing against the running system as opposed to testing code in isolation, usually by calling functions directly.

Isolated tests of code in a system using .NET Aspire do not need to differ from unit tests for any other type of application or system. It's for the broader tests against the running systems and processes that .NET Aspire provides the included test project templates.

Regardless of which test framework you choose, any of these templates will create a project, leveraging a popular and widely used test framework with setup provided for you for running your distributed system via a reference to the package *Aspire.Hosting.Testing*. To get up and running quickly with tests leveraging your AppHost project, this package provides the *DistributedApplicationTestingBuilder* class.

In the same way that adding project references to your system process projects in the AppHost project generates a class to reference that project in building your app model in the AppHost's *Program.cs*, adding a reference to your AppHost project in your Aspire test project generates a class to reference to start your AppHost.

In the end, this looks like the following:

- Create a .NET Aspire Test project

- Add a reference to the AppHost project to the test project

- Use code like *var appHost = await DistributedApplicationTestingBuilder .CreateAsync<Projects.AspireApp_AppHost>();* to create an instance of the builder for your distributed application to test against

- Build the distributed system with code like *app = await appHost.BuildAsync();*

- Arrange, act, and assert to test your distributed system

There is much more to say about writing integration tests for distributed systems. A later chapter will dive much further into testing with .NET Aspire.

Dependencies Between Application Code Projects

As we saw with the starter templates, project references are straightforward in .NET Aspire solutions. In most cases, your AppHost project will reference the application process projects you want to run when your distributed system runs. It uses code generation on project references to make a project something that can be referenced from code via the *Projects* namespace.

Your application process projects will then have references to the service defaults project to make use of the goodness of being able to easily set up cross-cutting concerns with that *builder.AddServiceDefaults()* extension method.

Service discovery, as set up in service defaults, will then take care of the rest. Your projects that serve as process endpoints will not typically need to reference one another and any communication they need to do with one another will be via message queues, calls over HTTP, or other types of RPC that will be configured using service discovery. These communications references and setups are done via the app model created in the AppHost project. Additionally, dependencies on other running software components, such as databases, are also made known in the app model, usually leveraging containers via integrations. As such, the dependency graph of project dependencies doesn't need to be very complex, though you'll likely have some class library projects in your solutions referenced by potentially many of your other projects and test projects will also have reference to the code they test.

Nonproject Resources

There are several types of resources you can add to your app model that are not .NET projects. Many of these can be done via integrations. Integrations can make a resource available in a cloud provider environment, in a container, hosting language runtime and executing code, or even just running a process.

Integrations aren't the only way to run nonproject resources. You can run containerized workloads by adding a container image to your app model or referencing a Dockerfile. A Dockerfile is a set of instructions for building a container image, so the ability to use a Dockerfile allows you to create custom images and run them straightforwardly when you run your app host. There's a lot of flexibility here for designing systems using the best tool for any individual job, and with the ability to use a Dockerfile, you can package just about anything into an image. You can add containers from images or from Dockerfiles with *builder.AddContainer()* and *builder.AddDockerfile()*, respectively. This documentation for including Dockerfiles is quite useful: https://learn.microsoft.com/dotnet/aspire/app-host/withdockerfile.

Another resource worth mentioning is the dashboard provided by Aspire. It's a useful tool for development on your workstation. That's what it's designed for, but it might be useful in other environments as well. It runs automatically with app host projects but is also available on its own. Even if you're not using .NET at all and not using an app host, you can integrate running the Aspire dashboard into applications built with other languages and platforms. Or, alternatively, you could run the dashboard without using .NET Aspire and send telemetry to it. It's an OpenTelemetry endpoint that can be run independently and can receive input from any process that sends OpenTelemetry information to it. If you want to find out more, visit https://aspiredashboard.com/. This site describes how to run the dashboard in a container and has samples of setting up programs in multiple languages to send OpenTelemetry.

Solution and Project Templates

In Chapter 2, we dove into using some of the *dotnet new* templates for
.NET Aspire. Here, I'll list all the templates (as of the time of writing) and
say a little about what they are and what purpose they serve. You can
always query for the template installed on your machine by using

```
$ dotnet new list aspire
```

These are the templates you should see:

- .NET Aspire App Host (aspire-apphost)

- .NET Aspire Empty App (aspire)

- .NET Aspire Service Defaults (aspire-servicedefaults)

- .NET Aspire Starter App (aspire-starter)

- .NET Aspire Test Project (MSTest) (aspire-mstest)

- .NET Aspire Test Project (NUnit) (aspire-nunit)

- .NET Aspire Test Project (xUnit) (aspire-xunit)

Two of them are solution templates, and the rest are all project
templates. We'll walk through them one by one.

*.NET Aspire App Host (*short name: aspire-apphost) is a project
template that creates an app host project. This is useful when you want to
add Aspire to an existing solution. Visual Studio and Visual Studio Code
have graphical tools that can create Aspire projects and add references to
orchestrate existing projects, so you might use that instead of using this
template directly. Chapter 9 has more on the graphical tools that can help
with this.

.NET Aspire Empty App (short name: aspire) is a solution template
that creates a new solution with only the two projects that are specific to
.NET Aspire: the app host and the service defaults. This is a blank solution

that has only the .NET Aspire bare bones to get started and to which you'll add your own projects and resources for implementing the meat of your system.

.NET Aspire Service Defaults (short name: aspire-servicedefaults) is a project template that creates a service defaults project with a default Extensions.cs static class. Like the aspire=apphost template, it's useful for adding Aspire to an existing solution and you can get this project from tooling in IDEs and editors such that you may not want to instantiate it directly. Chapter 9 has more on the graphical tools that can help with this.

.NET Aspire Starter App (short name: aspire-starter) is a solution template that creates a sample system with projects representing an API and a web frontend (and, optionally, a Redis integration and/or a test project). It's useful for getting acquainted with .NET Aspire and seeing what it can do. It can also be a starting point for a system you'll build if you want to include projects matching what it provides (though you'll probably want to delete some of the sample code).

.NET Aspire Test Project (MSTest) (short name: aspire-mstest) is a project template for creating a test project for tests that interact with your running system, using the MSTest testing framework.

.NET Aspire Test Project (NUnit) (short name: aspire-nunit) is a project template for creating a test project for tests that interact with your running system, using the NUnit testing framework.

.NET Aspire Test Project (xUnit) (short name: aspire-xunit) is a project template for creating a test project for tests that interact with your running system, using the xUnit testing framework.

Summary

This chapter focuses on the types of projects and resources composing a .NET Aspire system. There is a great deal of diversity of resources and flexibility for choosing the tools that fit best for what you need. The Aspire dashboard is a useful monitor for understanding your system on your workstation. It runs automatically with an app host but can also be executed independently.

The next chapter will discuss the architectural concerns that go into designing distributed systems with .NET Aspire.

CHAPTER 4

System Architecture Considerations

In prior chapters, we've looked at what .NET Aspire is and how to use it. These things are important to know. It's even more important to make sure what you're building with Aspire is going to suit the needs of the problem you're trying to solve.

This means you need to consider who will be using your system, both human users and API consumers. You need to think about usage patterns, scaling considerations, timing, elasticity of the demands on your system, security, and more.

The overall design of a distributed system needs to account for the big picture of what pieces make up the broader system and how those pieces fit together. These decisions can only be made in the context of knowing the problem to be solved, the constraints under which the software must execute, and the patterns of the demands on the system in times of light, typical, and heavy use.

This broad set of concerns, constraints, and designs makes up the considerations of how a system is architected. .NET Aspire is helpful in providing the app host project as an orchestrator to articulate the app model, which brings disparate pieces of the system interactions together.

To understand system architecture and how Aspire relates to it, we need to think about the nature of distributed systems, ways of designing systems, demands, and how we structure our source code.

© Dave Rael 2025
D. Rael, *Getting Started with .NET Aspire*, https://doi.org/10.1007/979-8-8688-1521-8_4

Named Architecture Patterns and the CAP Theorem

Software systems design can take many forms, and there are patterns that are tried and true for ways of approaching design to take into account the needs of distributed systems.

Systems running in networked environments are systems with multiple resources and failure of some of those resources is inevitable. The more resources enlisted, the more chances there are that something will not remain functional.

Eric Brewster presented a conjecture decades ago that would later become known as the CAP Theorem. You can find more about the CAP Theorem at `https://en.wikipedia.org/wiki/CAP_theorem`. CAP stands for consistency, availability, and partition tolerance. The idea was that there are limitations to the extent to which one can make guarantees of a distributed computer system. The main guarantees one desires can be articulated as consistency, availability, and partition tolerance. Brewster argued that only two of the three can be fully guaranteed at a time with compromises necessary on the third. This need for compromise is due to the need for reliability on top of unreliable resources and networking that can fail.

Entire books have been written about the compromises needed in designing systems to be resilient in the face of unreliable networks, storage, and computing. I'll not go deeply into arguing about why Brewster was correct in his conjecture but will rather point out that much of software architecture has been built on working through these design problems and making the necessary compromises in ways that serve the needs of software users and businesses.

Systems designed with the unreliability of networked cloud resources in mind are often created with composition from autonomous pieces with liberty within individual parts to design the pieces in ways that work in that context, with other areas designed differently.

Thus, the top-level architecture of distributed systems can take an approach setting out for autonomy within what Eric Evans called "bounded contexts" in his book, *Domain-Driven Design Tackling Complexity in the Heart of Software* (2003).

Designing for the autonomy of bounded contexts is what led to the movement known as service-oriented architecture (SOA). The main principle of service orientation is system composition from individual "services." The definition of what is a service differs greatly from one practitioner to another and is not something I'll address here.

Microservices is another approach to system architecture, often seen as an outgrowth of service-oriented architecture. The boundaries between what constitutes a system that is service-oriented vs. microservices are often articulated as being primarily about the size and scope of services, and there is fuzziness in the distinctions.

Characterizing a system as service-oriented, microservices, or something else is an important part of thinking about your designs. Microservices is a popular approach for a reason, and if you're not thinking about the autonomy of your bounded contexts, fault tolerance, and how you deploy, you should be. Microservices is an advanced architectural approach that has advantages, but it's not right for every situation. It often adds complexity that might not be justified, and it's hard to do well without experienced architects and developers designing the services and boundaries.

The popularity of microservices and level of buzz has led to a situation where a lot of distributed systems development gets conflated with microservices and many of the results for Internet searches you'll find might use the term microservice to refer to any process in a distributed system. This loose use of the term does lead to a lot of words written making it seem that .NET Aspire is something that is only for microservices architectures.

Is Aspire Only for Microservices?

There are many opinions on what microservices means and why the pattern is useful.

You might hear .NET Aspire called a toolset for microservices or something of the sort. It's true that if you are using microservices, the benefits of .NET Aspire apply and can make your development experience a lot more pleasant. It's not necessary, though, that you use a microservices approach to get benefit from .NET Aspire.

It is usually true that microservices systems are distributed systems, but it's not necessarily true that distributed systems need to follow a microservices approach.

A deep dive into what microservices is and is not is outside the scope of this book, but I can say that microservices is broadly an approach with the intent of composing a multifaceted system of individual and autonomous services that can be built, tested, and deployed in isolation and without dependencies on other services. Independent design, development, testing, and deployment is the name of the game with microservices. It's a valuable contribution to the ways we think about distributed systems.

Many designs of distributed systems, whether they claim to follow the microservices pattern or not, don't have system components that live up to these characteristics of services.

There are many opinions on the proper sizing of services in a microservices architecture and what form they should take. In short, many who claim to be doing microservices may not really be adhering to what microservices provide.

Ultimately, arguments over the nature of microservices aren't relevant to the topic at hand in this book. Whether you use a microservices architecture or not and whether your services really live up to what microservices should be are topics for a different discussion.

.NET Aspire may be useful for you if you are building distributed systems, microservices or not. That's the key: having multiple components of your system that need to run in separate processes, including both your custom software processes and dependencies like databases and message queueing resources. With multiple resources, you have a distributed system. It's not important to the question of using .NET Aspire whether your design fits the prescriptions of microservices.

In other words, .NET Aspire is for microservices, but it's not *only* for microservices.

When Is .NET Aspire Not Appropriate?

Generally, distributed systems development in .NET benefits from .NET Aspire. If what you are building is simply a single application process, you probably don't need Aspire. Most systems do have more than a single process, though, so Aspire is probably useful in most systems. There is such a thing as software that runs on a single machine, stores any useful information locally, and doesn't have any dependencies. Such an application will probably not benefit from .NET Aspire. If your system uses any sort of resources that are external to your application process, though, such as a database, you are arguably into the realm of simple distributed systems. Even just using a database, you can ease your development effort by using Aspire to be able to quickly, easily, and repeatably set up your database dependency by leveraging service discovery and containers or cloud resources from your development workstation.

This means that .NET Aspire can be useful in all but the simplest of .NET systems. It might even be useful, especially the dashboard, in systems not using .NET. Of course, you'll have to make the decisions for yourself as to what does and doesn't make sense in any given situation.

Source Repository Choices

Building software involves interacting with code under source control. The structure of how systems are designed and where the source code lives for the pieces that make up the whole of a distributed system is a source of contention. While the choices you make regarding version control are not really questions of system architecture, how you work in your organization, how you structure your teams, and how you store and structure your code have an influence on the designs you create.

Mel Conway articulated the notion of the influence of organization structures on systems design as what would come to be known as *Conway's Law*.

> *Organizations which design systems are constrained to pro-*
> *duce designs which are copies of the communication struc-*
> *tures of these organizations.*
>
> —Melvin E. Conway, How Do Committees Invent?

Given this reality, how you store, version, access, and work with your code is relevant to how you design your systems.

There are many who believe a "monorepo" (one large source repository with the source for many or all system components in one place) is a superior approach to building complex systems, while others like to take a "multirepo" or "polyrepo" path (discrete, dedicated repositories for each of the individual pieces or smaller sets of them). There are good reasons on both sides of the debate to choose one or another, and there is not a wrong or right answer.

Having the source of all pieces of a system in one repository simplifies the landscape for what developers need to do to get up and running with your code. New team members can clone a single repository and have everything at their fingertips. It also makes managing dependencies more straightforward. Rather than having considerations for managing packages and versions of different components, the source can always be referenced directly and straightforwardly.

Smaller repositories with subsets of your system also have advantages. Pipelines in automated build, test, and deployment systems can be simpler because they don't have to do as much filtering on what changes necessitate runs for given components. Packaging dependencies might be desirable anyway to make sure versioning is treated properly. Giving team members different access to different pieces of the system is also much more straightforward with different projects potentially having different sets of maintainers. Reading a changelog is simplified with different repositories, also, because more of the log is relevant to a given part of the system.

Generally, I prefer to have repositories dedicated to autonomous pieces of systems with a changelog showing only what has changed in that system. Working with .NET Aspire, though, does push a bit in the direction of larger repositories encompassing whole systems.

A part of the main value proposition of .NET Aspire is having the AppHost project orchestrate your system, and it does this best by having project references to the projects that make up the system processes in your environment. Project references work with source code sitting on a path on the filesystem easily referenced locally. This means you want to have the code for the different pieces together. So, if your preference is to use a monorepo, rejoice. .NET Aspire works nicely with such a setup.

If you, like me, prefer to use discreet repositories, there are ways you can still do it, but there are limitations to how well it works.

.NET Aspire with a Multirepo Setup

In this section, I'll describe a handful of options for how you can approach having multiple repositories with .NET Aspire and demonstrate the one I prefer in detail. If you use a monorepo and know you'll only be using a monorepo, you could skip this section and proceed to the next chapter, unless you are curious about this.

One option for a distributed system with sources of different elements in different repositories is to have an app model in each subsystem that runs that subsystem as a project and the others as containers. If you have a continuous integration system producing container images of each version of your software and pushing them to a registry, you can straightforwardly reference those images to build up an app model. This approach has the limitation that if you want to change something in one of the other subsystems, it's not as straightforward just changing the code and continuing like it is with having the code in the same repository.

Another approach is to have a standard for relative paths for where you clone the repositories. If you do this, you can have your AppHost in a repository for the system and have it reference the other projects via relative paths that point outside that repository with the expectation that the other repositories will be cloned to predictable paths. There are many ways this can go wrong and can lead to troubleshooting, but a standard enshrined in a script that clones everything to the expected relative paths could make this reliable. With these different clones lying around keeping them all up to date can be something that requires some effort.

Yet another option is an interesting NuGet package to enable adding project resources to an AppHost using a repository URL. (`https://github.com/Dutchskull/Aspire.PolyRepo`) This enables you to add a repository resource to your app model, add projects from the repository, and put the AppHost in charge of cloning your repository and checking out the snapshot you want to use. This is an idea with merit. I've not used it, though. My experience with using multiple repositories has been to use the method below of using Git submodules. The notion of referencing a repository by URL in the app model has intrigued me, though, and I'd like to give it a try.

Also, among the options for using a .NET Aspire AppHost with multiple repositories is the use of Git submodules. If you have different solutions in different repositories that you want to run together in a distributed system, you can have your AppHost project in a repository of its own (or coupled with something that might be considered a main service or something of the sort) and include the other repositories with the use of submodules.

Git submodules allow one repository to reference another. Essentially, when you create a submodule, you commit a configuration setup that references another repository such that when you check out a snapshot in the referencing repository, you're also checking out a snapshot from the referenced repository. I usually try to avoid submodules because they require some maintenance to make them work the way you want. Updating the commit pointed to by the parent repository can get a little hairy. They fit nicely, though, with the use case of wanting to have projects making up a system live in different repositories.

There are downsides to using submodules. It can be confusing to deal with different commits in different repositories and making sure all of the changes to all of the repositories get pushed to central server repositories. Fetching, pulling, and pushing changes can confuse team members even without submodules, and the added complexity of dealing with multiple repositories with references to one another increases this hazard. Teams can be also impacted if references to commits in the root repository are pushed without pushing the commit in the submodule repository. There are pitfalls, but it's an approach that works well if you want to have subsystems in different repositories.

Note   Mercurial also has a feature called subrepositories that works similarly to Git submodules if you're using Mercurial instead of Git.

An Example of .NET Aspire with a Multirepo Setup Using Git Submodules

Let's build a sample of what it might look like to create a system setup with different repositories for different elements of a system. I'll use Git and Git submodules to make this work. If you don't use Git or don't want to use submodules for a multirepo setup, you could skip this section and proceed to the next chapter, unless you're curious about this. It does assume you know something about Git, which is usually a pretty good assumption in current software development work.

Let's say we want to build a system composed of two autonomous services. Without better names for what the services should do, let's call them orange and yellow. Because these services are autonomous and should be able to run on their own and I want the teams maintaining them to have maintainer permissions on their own subsystem but only be able to submit pull requests to the other, I'll put them in different repositories. Further, I'll create separate repositories for my .NET Aspire service defaults project and for the system as a whole (which will contain the AppHost orchestrator project and a project for end-to-end testing).

I could demonstrate using repositories as submodules with repositories only on my local filesystem, but you'll generally be dealing with repositories on a server with which you interact with your team, so I'll create my samples using GitHub repositories as the source for the submodules. GitHub is a service that offers both free and paid plans for hosting Git repositories with web tools for interacting with them in addition to setting them up as remotes for your local Git repositories. This will probably be more straightforward to understand. It does not have to be GitHub. Really, any Git repository would do. If you'd rather use a different source control provider, you can do essentially the same thing in any of them.

I'll start by creating three GitHub repositories named servicedefaults, orange, and yellow. In a real system, I'd also create one for my system repository, but for our purposes here, that's not necessary as it will not be referenced as a submodule and GitHub won't be needed for this demonstration. I'll just have it as a local repository on my filesystem.

To do this exercise, log into your GitHub account if you have one. If you don't, you can create a free account on https://github.com.

I suggest creating an organization to namespace these projects and not pollute your user namespace. This also enables you to do something like this exercise more than once in the same way, confined to an organization. If you would rather just create repositories under your user instead of in an organization, you can certainly do that.

Create the organization by using the "+" dropdown in the top left of the GitHub user interface and selecting "New organization".

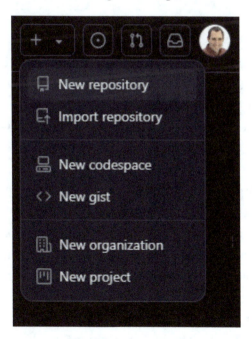

Figure 4-1. *GitHub options menu for creating new resources*

Then choose the "Create a free organization" option.

Figure 4-2. *GitHub free organization option*

Give your organization a name and email address and associate it with your personal account and continue by clicking "Next". I'm naming my organization "RaelAspireMultirepo". Yours will need to be something different, as these names need to be unique across all of GitHub. Then click the green "Complete Setup" button on the next page and you have an organization.

Within the organization, click the "Create new repository" button. In the scope of your organization, name the first repository "servicedefaults". Check the box for "Add a README file". Adding this repository as a submodule is a lot more straightforward if it already has a commit, and checking this checkbox will make sure the repository starts with a commit. Click "Create repository" (or press the Enter key).

Now, click on the name of your organization on the top right of the GitHub website to go back to the organization. You should again be able to add another repository and will do the same thing, with a different name.

Within the organization, click the "Create new repository" button. In the scope of your organization, name the next repository orange. Check the box for "Add a README file". Adding this repository as a submodule is a lot more straightforward if it already has a commit, and checking this checkbox will make sure the repository starts with a commit. Click "Create repository" (or press the Enter key).

Now, click on the name of your organization on the top right of the GitHub website to go back to the organization. You should again be able to add another repository and will do the same thing, with a different name.

Within the organization, click the "Create new repository" button. In the scope of your organization, name the next repository yellow. Check the box for "Add a README file". Adding this repository as a submodule is a lot more straightforward if it already has a commit, and checking this checkbox will make sure the repository starts with a commit. Click "Create repository" (or press the Enter key).

You should now have a GitHub organization with three projects. We'll go back to your filesystem to create the system repository on disk. From it, we'll add submodules for the subsystem repositories.

Start on your filesystem in a directory where you are creating your demonstration exercise repositories.

The following will create a top-level directory for the system root repository and turn it into a Git repository.

```
$ mkdir system
$ cd system
$ git init
```

Also, add a .NET-specific *.gitignore* file to prevent committing generated files that shouldn't get committed and to reduce noise in viewing *git status*.

```
$ dotnet new gitignore
```

Now, we'll start by creating a .NET solution.

```
$ dotnet new sln
```

Let's create our system AppHost project and add it to the solution as well.

```
$ dotnet new aspire-apphost -o AppHost
$ dotnet sln add AppHost
```

And we'll create a project for running end-to-end tests against the whole running system (I like xUnit, your preference may be different) and add it to the solution.

```
$ dotnet new aspire-xunit -o Test
$ dotnet sln add Test
```

The test project will need to have a reference to the AppHost project to run the whole system in the testing context.

```
$ dotnet add Test reference AppHost
```

Now, the top-level projects are set up for an AppHost. It's a boring AppHost that doesn't yet have any resources to run, but it's a start. Running the AppHost at this point would indeed launch the app and run the dashboard, but there's not much reason to get excited about that. You can try it if you like.

It's a good idea to at least do a *dotnet build* just to make sure packages restore and the solution builds successfully.

This minimal setup now has a directory structure that looks like the following.

Figure 4-3. Root directory of the system repository before adding submodules

With the solution building, it's a good time to create a starting commit in the repository.

```
$ git add .
$ git commit -m "Start solution for multirepo system"
```

The next thing I want to do is to add a Git submodule so we can create a project to include as a project resource in the AppHost we just created. If my GitHub organization repository URL path is *https://github.com/RaelAspireMultirepo/*, I'll be able to reach my repositories via SSH at git@github.com:RaelAspireMultirepo/servicedefaults.git, git@github.com:RaelAspireMultirepo/orange.git, and git@github.com:RaelAspireMultirepo/yellow.git.

Note I'll be using Secure Shell (SSH) URLs. GitHub treats these as default (though they have gone back and forth over the years on SSH vs. HTTPS being default), and I prefer to use them and it's more straightforward to do so on platforms other than Windows. It's also arguably a bit more secure than using HTTPS. Git on Windows has a nice built-in and enabled-by-default credential manager such that using HTTPS is pretty easy and seamless with entering your password once and having Windows remember it. You can set up credentials managers on Linux and Mac for use with Git over HTTPS, but it's better and easier, in my mind, to just use SSH. SSH does require setting up a public key with your GitHub (or whatever source hosting service you use) account for authentication. If you find this confusing and/or you're using Windows and/or you typically use HTTPS repository URLs, you should use HTTPS.

Knowing these SSH locations for my server repositories, I can add a submodule, starting with the orange service, to clone my orange repository into my system repository. If you're not already familiar with submodules, there's quite a bit here that will be new. It's a simple idea, but it doesn't obviously fit with intuition, at least for me. Add the submodule like this (you'll want to use the path to the repository in your organization, not mine):

```
$ git submodule add git@github.com:RaelAspireMultirepo/
orange.git
```

To see what has just happened with this command, let's look at what Git tells us has changed:

```
$ git status
On branch main
Changes to be committed:
  (use "git restore --staged <file>..." to unstage)
        new file:   .gitmodules
        new file:   orange
```

A new file was created and so was a new subdirectory (though *git status* shows it as a file). We can see that orange is in fact a directory:

Figure 4-4. *Root directory of the system repository after adding the orange repository as a submodule*

The content of the new hidden file that Git wrote to disk, .gitmodules, looks like this:

```
[submodule "orange"]
        path = orange
        url = git@github.com:RaelAspireMultirepo/orange.git
```

This tells us that we've created a submodule and where the origin repository for it can be found. If we ask Git to show us the diff for the directory representing the submodule, it will tell us about the commit it is referencing there.

```
$ git diff --cached orange
diff --git a/orange b/orange
new file mode 160000
index 0000000..22909e5
--- /dev/null
+++ b/orange
@@ -0,0 +1 @@
+Subproject commit 22909e59801a046f6a4bddfcc000b10b7fe530ca
```

The last line is the part that tells us the interesting bit. It shows the hash of the commit the main repository is referencing. This means the subrepisotry is a reference to a specific commit identified by this hash. This leads to a checkout of the orange submodule as a reference to a repository, and it has checked out a specific commit in that repository in the subdirectory that is a working directory for that repository. In fact, if we change our terminal context to the subdirectory, we can work in the submodule as a proper git repository itself. We want to do just that, but in a moment. First, we want to commit the addition of the submodule. Unlike changes to the files in your working directory, the addition of the submodule is automatically added to the index (staged for commit), so a *git add* is not necessary here.

```
$ git commit -m "Add orange service as a submodule to enable
app model add"
```

Now, let's move into the *orange* subdirectory, which is the working directory for the orange repository associated with the submodule. *Git status* will show us that this is indeed a Git repository and we're on a branch with a tracking relationship to a remote branch.

```
$ cd orange
$ git status
On branch main
Your branch is up to date with 'origin/main'.

nothing to commit, working tree clean
```

Looking at the history of this repository reflects the same changelog as that on the GitHub server for the orange project (a single commit that resulted from checking the checkbox to include a README file).

```
$ git log
commit 22909e59801a046f6a4bddfcc000b10b7fe530ca (HEAD -> main,
origin/main, origin/HEAD)
```

Author: Dave Rael
Date: Sat Feb 8 18:15:40 2025 -0700

    Initial commit

This repository also has a remote pointing back to the GitHub project.

```
$ git remote -v
origin  git@github.com:RaelAspireMultirepo/orange.git (fetch)
origin  git@github.com:RaelAspireMultirepo/orange.git (push)
```

So here, we can go ahead and create a .NET project to include in our distributed system, and we'll be able to reference it in the AppHost project and add it to our app model. I'll just use the *webapi* template for this project because it's relatively small and simple and we can imagine that we'd like to have an API for our service. Given that whatever we do in this service repository, we'll want to test, I'll go ahead and create a unit test project as well and a solution for working with just his service, as well as a .gitignore for .NET.

```
$ dotnet new gitignore
$ dotnet new sln
$ dotnet new xunit -o Test
$ dotnet sln add Test
$ dotnet new webapi -o Api
$ dotnet sln add Api
$ dotnet add Test reference Api
```

This set of commands has quickly given us a new solution in this service repository in which we can flesh out this independent and autonomous (if we design it that way) service. At this point, we have working code that provides an API and we're ready to make a commit and get back to enlisting this project in our distributed system.

Figure 4-5. *The directory content of the orange directory – a Git repository resulting from the inclusion as a submodule*

```
$ git add .
$ git commit -m "Start orange service with tests and API"
```

Now that there's code committed in our submodule, let's go back up to the system repository and see if anything has changed.

```
$ cd ..
$ git status
On branch main
Changes not staged for commit:
  (use "git add <file>..." to update what will be committed)
  (use "git restore <file>..." to discard changes in working
  directory)
        modified:   orange (new commits)

no changes added to commit (use "git add" and/or "git
commit -a")
```

Just by adding a commit in the repository represented by the submodule, we've created a change in the referencing repository. This is how submodules work. Moving the checked out branch forward will cause the submodule reference to point to the new commit. This time, the change is not staged, so we'll have to add it to commit. We can commit this change to the system repository also (either in an isolated commit or we could go ahead and do what we're going to do with referencing the new project in the AppHost first – I prefer smaller, more targeted commits, so I'll go ahead and commit this updated commit reference). First, let's see the nature of the change:

```
$ git diff
diff --git a/orange b/orange
index 22909e5..c5a0b96 160000
--- a/orange
+++ b/orange
@@ -1 +1 @@
-Subproject commit 22909e59801a046f6a4bddfcc000b10b7fe530ca
+Subproject commit c5a0b967b62d8a8505867bb6de5ced009899c06d
```

This truly reflects just moving the commit referenced in the submodule, so let's add and commit it.

```
$ git add .
$ git commit -m "Move orange submodule forward to commit
with code"
```

We're now able to go ahead and add a reference to the orange service API project in the AppHost and have it start when we start the system orchestrator.

```
$ dotnet add AppHost reference orange/Api
```

While we're at it, let's go ahead and add the project to the solution as well.

```
$ dotnet sln add orange/Api
```

Recall that, in a .NET Aspire app host project, adding a reference to a .NET project triggers code generation such that there's now a class that can be used to include this project in the app model in the *Program.cs* file in the AppHost project itself.

We can add a line in the very sparse Program.cs app model file that looks like this before the change:

```
var builder = DistributedApplication.CreateBuilder(args);
builder.Build().Run();
```

And we'll make it look like this after the change:

```
var builder = DistributedApplication.CreateBuilder(args);
builder.AddProject<Projects.Api>("orangeapi");
builder.Build().Run();
```

Now, there's a project enlisted in our distributed application. At this point, running the AppHost with *dotnet run –project AppHost* will result in a resource showing on the dashboard because this WebApi project we created is a part of the app model.

Figure 4-6. *.NET Aspire dashboard showing a single resource from a multirepo setup using Git submodules*

Sending a request to the orange service API on the */weatherforecast* path will result in a successful response.

This is a good time to go ahead and create a commit to make a new snapshot of the system in this working state.

```
$ git add .
$ git commit -m "Include Orange Api in app model"
```

Though we have a working process now running, it's worth noticing that if you look at the dashboard and go to the structured logs, the traces, or the metrics, there's not any output there.

Figure 4-7. *.NET Aspire dashboard with empty structured logs without using service defaults*

Figure 4-8. *.NET Aspire dashboard with empty traces without using service defaults*

Figure 4-9. *.NET Aspire dashboard with empty metrics without using service defaults*

Console logging does appear.

Figure 4-10. *.NET Aspire dashboard with console logs without using service defaults*

There's a reason for this. The console logging is simply the directing of console output that will happen one way or another to the dashboard, but the other telemetry is output that needs to be set up explicitly and with dependencies on packages that make for output compatible with OpenTelemetry. It's via the extensions of the ServiceDefaults project that our prior efforts made those things work. Using the defaults will be good enough to see this in the dashboard, so let's go ahead and create a service defaults project from the template.

This is a spot where I'm going to diverge from what I'd do in a real project using a multirepo strategy with Git submodules. Ideally, it would be nice to just have the service defaults in the repository with the AppHost project, but it doesn't work that way. You may have been wondering why I created a separate repository for the service defaults. The reason is that the dependency graph with .NET Aspire is such that the processes for which we write application code need to reference the service defaults project. You have a chain of AppHost ➤ application process project ➤ service defaults.

In a real project, I'd use a repository for my service defaults project and set it up to produce a NuGet package and use a pipeline to build the package and push it to a NuGet registry. My expectation is that this package would change infrequently. Once the team establishes the standards for the system for health checks, service discovery, and telemetry, this package would just be used without having to do updates most of the time.

Because this book is not really about packages and pushing to registries, it seems that's more of a tangent than something useful to include here. It could be argued that so are Git submodules, but if you want to use Aspire with multiple repositories for different services, it's something I think you want to at least consider. If you'd like to find more information about hosting a NuGet feed, pushing your packages to it, and using it as a source, there's a Microsoft documentation page that serves as a hub for several offerings that make package feeds available with links to detail on setting up any of them (`https://learn.microsoft.com/nuget/hosting-packages/overview`). I'm generally fond of using the feeds built into the source hosting platforms, like GitHub package registry, GitLab Package Registry, Azure Artifacts, etc.

Because producing a package is probably more distraction than help here, I'll go ahead and add the service defaults repository as a submodule in the orange repository, creating a layered submodule structure. In this way, we can create a reference on the project we'll create for service defaults in the WebApi project we've already created.

Now, I want to go back into the orange subdirectory to interact with that repository.

```
$ cd orange
```

In there, I'll add the submodule.

```
$ git submodule add git@github.com:RaelAspireMultirepo/
servicedefaults.git
```

This will have a similar result to the prior adding of the orange service repository as a submodule, and we can go ahead and commit this already staged change in the orange repository.

```
$ git commit -m "Add service defaults as a submodule

to be able to use standard setup for useful concerns"
```

We can move into the new servicedefaults subdirectory, which is a repository itself.

```
$ cd servicedefaults
```

Now, let's go ahead and create the project. It's arguable whether you'd want to create a project for unit tests for your service defaults. In this case, I'll just decide I'm not going to do that. If you do want to create such tests, you'd probably want to create a solution and put projects into subdirectories. Here, I won't bother with that and will just create a .NET-flavored .gitignore and put the project in the root of this repository.

```
$ dotnet new gitignore
$ dotnet new aspire-servicedefaults
```

Given that here we're just going to use the defaults provided by .NET Aspire, let's just commit this and be done with it.

```
$ git add .
$ git commit -m "Add service defaults to standardize"
```

It's also a good idea to push this to the remote, because if we take the same approach in the yellow service and add the service defaults as a submodule, we'll want it to be there on GitHub.

```
$ git push
```

Now, we're ready to move back up into the orange repository and reference and use this new project.

```
$ cd ..
```

Before using it, though, I'll commit the updated reference to the new commit in the servicedefaults repository. As a reminder, *git status* will show that there's a submodule change and *git diff* will indicate what the change is (a new commit).

```
$ git diff --git a/servicedefaults b/servicedefaults
index c0a0d14..46fe648 160000
--- a/servicedefaults
+++ b/servicedefaults
@@ -1 +1 @@
-Subproject commit c0a0d14ce19262c7fc4c8d3c5b7e207558d02ade
+Subproject commit 46fe648ed5f2ac43ec2fefd0a7f8c0487a3d0ea2
```

This change needs to be added to the index before committing. It's only the adding of a new submodule that is automatically staged.

```
$ git add .
$ git commit -m "Move to service defaults commit with project"
```

The next step will be to create a reference to the project.

```
$ dotnet add Api reference servicedefaults
```

With the reference in place, we can call the extension method that is the main entry point for using .NET Aspire service defaults. This will involve adding a line to *Program.cs*. I'll not include the whole file for brevity, you'll just want to call *AddServiceDefaults()* on the WebApplicationBuilder right after it gets created (and certainly before *build()* gets called).

```
var builder = WebApplication.CreateBuilder(args);
builder.AddServiceDefaults();
```

You'll want to verify that you're able to build successfully and might want to run either just the orange API or even the whole AppHost. When you're satisfied that this works, you'll want to go ahead and commit this update in the orange repository with two files changed – the *Api.csproj* project file with the added reference and the Program.cs file with the call to add the service defaults to the builder.

```
$ git add .
$ git commit -m "Add service defaults for standard setup"
```

After committing, it's worth pushing to the GitHub remote as well.

```
$ git push
```

The service defaults project is now in place in the orange service Api project. It's time to go back up to the system level and run the system and see what we have (and commit the updated submodule).

```
$ cd ..
$ dotnet run -project AppHost
```

Running the app host now should look the same as before, except now you should find that the service defaults did the trick and you are now able to see structured logs, traces, and metrics (traces will only appear after you've made a request, as they are tracing an interaction through the whole life cycle, which is more interesting when the are some dependencies between the projects, which we don't have here – but they are showing up).

Figure 4-11. *.NET Aspire dashboard with structured logs due to using service defaults*

Figure 4-12. *.NET Aspire dashboard with traces due to using service defaults*

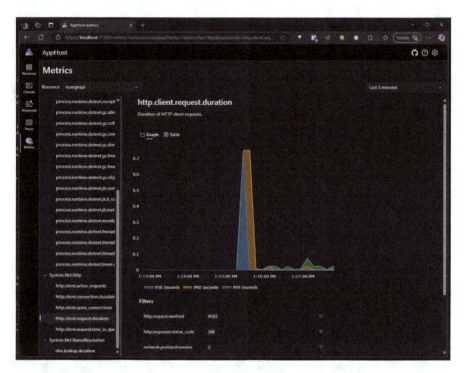

Figure 4-13. *.NET Aspire dashboard with metrics due to using service defaults*

Don't forget to commit the updated reference.

```
$ git add .
$ git commit -m "Move to service defaults commit with project"
```

The next step, at this point, in fleshing out our broader system is to include the yellow service like we did the orange. Because that will largely involve repetition, I'll leave that as an exercise for the reader, should you choose to accept it. There are a few things to note before doing that, though.

For one thing, this exercise, so far, has not included adding any dependencies between different projects in the system or any integrations. That could certainly be done. The starter solution template does give examples of how to do those things, so it should be straightforward to do that with a setup like this involving a system-wide solution with service repositories as submodules. More flesh on this example would probably involve some web user interface components as well. It's likely that individual services could have user interfaces and there may be a broader system user interface as well. You have many degrees of freedom in setting up your system in this way. One big repository with everything certainly can work well for such setups, but using submodules in this way is a useful approach if you want the repositories separated.

Also, I deliberately named the API project in the orange service *Api* instead of something like *Orange.Api* that disambiguates it in the broader system from something in another service. It's my preference to name things in a given bounded context for what it is within that context. Naming it differently with something that works across the system is an option, but if you're like me and like simpler naming within a service, you might expect to run into a problem with the code generation if you create a project in the yellow service with the same name. This is, indeed, a problem, but there's a simple resolution. The reference in the AppHost. csproj project file can take an additional attribute to control the name of the generated class for adding the project to the app model.

This looks like changing:

```
<ProjectReference Include="..\orange\Api\Api.csproj" />
```

to

```
<ProjectReference Include="..\orange\Api\Api.csproj" Aspire
ProjectMetadataTypeName="Orange_Api" />
```

and then changing, in the *Program.cs* (app model):

```
builder.AddProject<Projects.Api>("orangeapi");
```

to

```
builder.AddProject<Projects.Orange_Api>("orangeapi");
```

Using this attribute gives you control of the name of the class generated, which can be useful.

The one more thing I'd like to add about using submodules in this way is to acknowledge that all of this committing at multiple levels and committing the updated references to those commits might seem like a bit much. It's true that it's a lot to have to do. There is some relief, though, if you consider that you might make sure service defaults project into the package to reference, rather than a submodule. This means needing to version packages and deal with managing that, including having a feed available for your packages (all of the major source control providers do have built in package feeds). It simplifies the graph, though, of your submodules. Further, you don't necessarily need to do all of the updating of the system repository manually. You could have pipelines for the services that update the system repository with the latest versions for appropriate branches when there are updates. In short, much of it can be automated.

Summary

This chapter is primarily about how .NET Aspire relates to system architecture with some consideration for team dynamics and how that impacts system design and source repository choices.

Distributed systems architecture is a complex topic with many nuances. You must make sure you're building your system to solve the problem at hand and to deal with the load it will face. Cloud computing enables systems to respond to growing needs and to do so cost efficiently but comes with its own set of problems to deal with.

Named architecture patterns are useful in thinking about how your system should operate, scale, and segregate responsibilities. They do not necessarily change whether you do or don't need distributed systems. In all but the simplest of cases, your modern software systems will indeed be distributed and will likely benefit from .NET Aspire.

.NET Aspire works seamlessly with monorepo source code structures. If you have a system with multiple repositories supporting a boarder whole, it will require some thought and effort to use an app model to run your whole system. You have some options. They all come with some compromises.

No matter what choices you make in your system architecture and code structure, you'll need to test your systems. The next chapter will address the testing of systems using .NET Aspire.

CHAPTER 5

Testing Your Systems

Effective software testing is what takes good software practice to the next level. Code that doesn't have good, automated tests is much harder to trust than code with tests that drive and assert the desired behavior of code and of the system.

.NET Aspire provides support for testing, but it may not be what you think. The testing support provided by Aspire is mainly for testing running systems, rather than testing functions and business logic in isolation.

.NET Aspire does not prevent testing units, but it really helps with testing broader systems.

Unit Testing with .NET Aspire

Generally, when you are writing unit tests for your distributed system, you are writing tests that are only testing a specific piece of code.

The term "unit" is a nonspecific term that can mean a lot of things, and I think this was deliberate to allow for a great deal of flexibility in the types of tests one can write and still call them unit tests.

Ideally, good unit tests are written against "pure" functions – functions that have no side effects and are comprised of deterministic mapping of input to output. A function is pure if it does not change any application state, and for the same input, it will always return the same output.

© Dave Rael 2025
D. Rael, *Getting Started with .NET Aspire*, https://doi.org/10.1007/979-8-8688-1521-8_5

When business logic is expressed with pure functions, tests are straightforward. One either writes tests for the range of all possible inputs or chooses meaningful examples that test the bounds of valid input and cases that are typical and/or representative of what will be used in the running system for a particular piece of logic.

Tests of pure functions are straightforward to write and to maintain, perform with reliable speed, and serve as a foundation for asserting the correctness of your system and its resistance to regression.

For these reasons, the best unit tests are tests that run easily in the context of a test runner and don't require any application processes running for their execution.

In short, they don't need your distributed system in a running state. This means that they don't need .NET Aspire.

For most unit testing, especially unit testing done well, you'll not need anything Aspire specific for your tests. You'll simply create a test project or a set of test projects using a testing framework you and your team prefer, reference your business logic and application process assemblies, and unit test as you would any system you've ever written before.

This is a book about .NET Aspire, and for the purposes of this work, saying that Aspire is mostly not relevant to your unit testing is enough.

Integration Testing with .NET Aspire

Not all tests are unit tests, though. Mike Cohn famously articulated what he called *the test automation pyramid*, which is also often called simply *the test pyramid*. The idea is that you have different types of tests of differing scope, scale, and speed and that you should have more tests that run faster and that are smaller in scope. These are the unit tests to provide you with the quickest feedback cycles during your daily development. Unit tests that run quickly give fast feedback to drive the continual process of creating software.

On top of that foundation of numerous fast tests, you should layer relatively fewer tests that run slower but have broader coverage for the integration of more pieces of your system. These tests do not provide feedback as quickly as your unit tests do, but they cover more pieces of your system working together and can uncover dysfunction in the interaction between units that unit testing alone can't cover.

Still slower and ideally less numerous, end-to-end (E2E) tests cover the system as a whole and make assertions on outcomes resulting from system-level interactions.

The distinctions between these types of tests can blur a bit in real life, but the idea is worth considering. In most systems, you're going to want to have a suite or suites of tests that cover more pieces together than just testing functions in isolation.

The testing support in .NET Aspire is intended to help with your integration and E2E tests by running your distributed system with your tests via the test runner process as a host for your AppHost project. For our purposes in this book, I'm not going to worry much about the distinction between integration tests and E2E tests and will just use the term integration test to refer to tests that run system processes and interact with those processes via defined protocols and make assertions about system outputs and system state rather than running units of code in a test runner process without any context of the execution of the system or its pieces. You might have a suite of integration tests that are testing more than just units, maybe using databases and other dependencies, but not necessarily running whole processes from your system. If so, please forgive me for using this terminology a little loosely.

.NET Aspire Test Projects

When we looked earlier at the solution and project templates provided by .NET Aspire, among them were some templates for test projects. To jog your memory, let's look again at the output of querying *dotnet new* for templates with *aspire* in the name.

```
$ dotnet new list aspire
These templates matched your input: 'aspire'

Template Name                     Short Name               Language
--------------------------------- ------------             --------
.NET Aspire App Host              aspire-apphost              [C#]
.NET Aspire Empty App             aspire                      [C#]
.NET Aspire Service Defaults      aspire-servicedefaults      [C#]
.NET Aspire Starter App           aspire-starter              [C#]
.NET Aspire Test Project (MSTest) aspire-mstest               [C#]
.NET Aspire Test Project (NUnit)  aspire-nunit                [C#]
.NET Aspire Test Project (xUnit)  aspire-xunit                [C#]
```

The last three of these templates are project templates for test projects. They differ from one another only in which popular .NET test frameworks they use. If you prefer any of MSTest, NUnit, or xUnit, you're in luck. .NET Aspire has a template using your choice of testing toolset.

In addition to these project templates, the starter solution template we looked at before includes an option for including a test project. I'll start diving into what we can do with test projects in .NET Aspire by creating a new starter solution and using the option to create a test project. This is like how I used the template with the option for including Redis for output caching, except that the option for including a test project takes a parameter of its own – one that chooses which test framework you'd like to use.

Thus, for including a test project with the starter template, you use an option and tell it which framework you'd like to use, and if you add a test project to an existing solution, you choose the test framework via the template that you choose. We'll look at both ways of creating a test project, starting with using the starter solution template.

.NET Aspire Starter Solution with Testing

Options for dotnet new templates can be specified from the command line when instantiating a project or solution from a template. They can also be given in the new project dialogs in integrated development environments like Visual Studio and Rider with controls like checkboxes and textboxes.

From the command line, creating a new .NET Aspire starter solution with a test project included, using the xUnit framework, looks like

```
$ dotnet new aspire-starter --test-framework xUnit.net -o
starter-with-test
The template ".NET Aspire Starter App" was created
successfully.
This template contains technologies from parties other than
Microsoft, see https://aka.ms/dotnet/aspire/third-party-notices
for details.

Processing post-creation actions...
Restoring /home/raelyard/code/aspire-book-code/starter-with-
test/starter-with-test.sln:
Restore succeeded.
Restoring /home/raelyard/code/aspire-book-code/starter-
with-test/starter-with-test.AppHost/starter-with-test.
AppHost.csproj:
Restore succeeded.
Restoring /home/raelyard/code/aspire-book-code/starter-with-
test/starter-with-test.ServiceDefaults/starter-with-test.
```

```
ServiceDefaults.csproj:
Restore succeeded.
Restoring /home/raelyard/code/aspire-book-code/starter-
with-test/starter-with-test.ApiService/starter-with-test.
ApiService.csproj:
Restore succeeded.
Restoring /home/raelyard/code/aspire-book-code/starter-with-
test/starter-with-test.Web/starter-with-test.Web.csproj:
Restore succeeded.
Restoring /home/raelyard/code/aspire-book-code/starter-with-
test/starter-with-test.Tests/starter-with-test.Tests.csproj:
Restore succeeded.
```

The output of this command is similar to what we saw before, but now has an additional project included. With the name I gave to the solution, the test project is called *starter-with-test.Tests* and is in a subdirectory with the same name.

Looking at the project file, *starter-with-test.Tests.csproj*, you will notice that the template automatically adds a reference to the AppHost project to the test project and you'll see packages you'd expect to see in a typical test project, in addition to one that is Aspire specific, `Aspire.Hosting.Testing`.

```
<Project Sdk="Microsoft.NET.Sdk">
  <PropertyGroup>
    <TargetFramework>net9.0</TargetFramework>
    <ImplicitUsings>enable</ImplicitUsings>
    <Nullable>enable</Nullable>
    <IsPackable>false</IsPackable>
    <IsTestProject>true</IsTestProject>
  </PropertyGroup>
```

```xml
<ItemGroup>
  <PackageReference Include="Aspire.Hosting.Testing"
  Version="9.0.0" />
  <PackageReference Include="coverlet.collector"
  Version="6.0.2" />
  <PackageReference Include="Microsoft.NET.Test.Sdk"
  Version="17.10.0" />
  <PackageReference Include="xunit" Version="2.9.0" />
  <PackageReference Include="xunit.runner.visualstudio"
  Version="2.8.2" />
</ItemGroup>

<ItemGroup>
  <ProjectReference Include="..\starter-with-test.AppHost\
  starter-with-test.AppHost.csproj" />
</ItemGroup>

<ItemGroup>
  <Using Include="System.Net" />
  <Using Include="Microsoft.Extensions.
  DependencyInjection" />
  <Using Include="Aspire.Hosting.ApplicationModel" />
  <Using Include="Aspire.Hosting.Testing" />
  <Using Include="Xunit" />
</ItemGroup>
</Project>
```

It's the *Aspire.Hosting.Testing* package that is unique to integration test project created with .NET Aspire. To understand what it provides, let's look at the sample test file created by the starter template with the test option exercised. In the *starter-with-test.Tests* directory, you should find a C# file called WebTests.cs. It looks like this:

```
namespace starter_with_test.Tests;

public class WebTests
{
    [Fact]
    public async Task GetWebResourceRootReturnsOkStatusCode()
    {
        // Arrange
        var appHost = await DistributedApplication
        TestingBuilder.CreateAsync<Projects.starter_with_test_
        AppHost>();
        appHost.Services.ConfigureHttpClientDefaults(client
        Builder =>
        {
            clientBuilder.AddStandardResilienceHandler();
        });
        // To output logs to the xUnit.net ITestOutputHelper,
            consider adding a package from https://www.nuget.
            org/packages?q=xunit+logging

        await using var app = await appHost.BuildAsync();
        var resourceNotificationService = app.Services.Get
        RequiredService<ResourceNotificationService>();
        await app.StartAsync();

        // Act
        var httpClient = app.CreateHttpClient("webfrontend");
        await resourceNotificationService.WaitForResource
```

```
Async("webfrontend", KnownResourceStates.Running).
    WaitAsync(TimeSpan.FromSeconds(30));
    var response = await httpClient.GetAsync("/");

    // Assert
    Assert.Equal(HttpStatusCode.OK, response.StatusCode);
    }
}
```

Your eye should be immediately drawn to the creation of a variable called appHost with an assignment to it from the return of a call to *DistributedApplicationTestingBuilder.CreateAsync<Projects.starter_with_ test_AppHost>()*. You may notice that the generic parameter looks similar to what we saw in the *Program.cs* of our AppHost project that results from code generation from project reference such that we were able to reference our application process projects from the AppHost project. Well, here, we're referencing our AppHost project from our test project. The .NET Aspire SDK code generation in the AppHost project works such that in addition to generating classes in the *Projects* namespace for types to reference our added projects, there's also a type for the AppHost itself. Thus, a generic type parameter can be used to create an instance of IDistributedApplicationTestingBuilder for the AppHost. This builder can then build an instance of *Aspire.Hosting.DistributedApplication*. This is the same type we build and run in the AppHost itself.

What all of this means is that, with the code in this sample test, you are running your distributed application when you run this test. In addition to that, service location is available in your test code such that you can create the likes of an HttpClient, as is done in this sample test, that is set up to make requests against constituent elements of your running system. In this case, the following code is creating a client, provided by the distributed application, that has the service discovery set up to talk to the resource registered with the distributed application (in the AppHost's Program.cs) as "webfrontend". This HttpClient instance is then useful for requesting any path in that running resource (in this case, "/" for the root of the web application).

```
var httpClient = app.CreateHttpClient("webfrontend");
await resourceNotificationService.WaitForResource
Async("webfrontend", KnownResourceStates.Running).
WaitAsync(TimeSpan.FromSeconds(30));
var response = await httpClient.GetAsync("/");
```

This provides powerful capabilities for being able to test that your system works together by making requests to websites and APIs, enqueueing messages, querying and/or mutating data, and more. You don't need to worry about ports and such – it's all there in the service discovery .NET Aspire is already doing for us.

Adding a .NET Aspire Test Project to an Existing Solution

In most cases, you won't be using the *aspire-starter* solution template in your real work. For this reason, you'll likely have either a new solution with the projects you need specifically for your system design or an existing solution already constructed with your system components. It may be the case that you're adding .NET Aspire to an existing system and want to include testing with it.

In Chapter 10, I'll give a more complete example of taking an existing system and adding .NET Aspire including the addition of an integration test project. For now, I'll use the *aspire-starter* template and create a new project without a testing project and then add one to it to see what that looks like.

As before, we can create a new solution from the command line with *dotnet new*.

```
$ dotnet new aspire-starter -o plain-starter-to-add-test
The template ".NET Aspire Starter App" was created
successfully.
This template contains technologies from parties other than
Microsoft, see https://aka.ms/dotnet/aspire/third-party-notices
for details.

Processing post-creation actions...
Restoring /home/raelyard/code/aspire-book-code/plain-starter-
to-add-test/plain-starter-to-add-test.sln:
Restore succeeded.
Restoring /home/raelyard/code/aspire-book-code/plain-starter-
to-add-test/plain-starter-to-add-test.AppHost/plain-starter-to-
add-test.AppHost.csproj:
Restore succeeded.
Restoring /home/raelyard/code/aspire-book-code/plain-starter-
to-add-test/plain-starter-to-add-test.ServiceDefaults/plain-
starter-to-add-test.ServiceDefaults.csproj:
Restore succeeded.
Restoring /home/raelyard/code/aspire-book-code/plain-starter-
to-add-test/plain-starter-to-add-test.ApiService/plain-starter-
to-add-test.ApiService.csproj:
Restore succeeded.
Restoring /home/raelyard/code/aspire-book-code/plain-starter-
to-add-test/plain-starter-to-add-test.Web/plain-starter-to-add-
test.Web.csproj:
Restore succeeded.
```

Now, change your directory context into the directory of the new solution.

```
$ cd plain-starter-to-add-test
```

To make clearer what has already happened and what happens when you add your new testing project to this already existing solution, let's make it more official that this already exists by creating a Git repository and committing what we've done with this creation. The first step to doing this successfully will be to also create a *.gitignore* file for the repository to get rid of all the noise of file generated by .NET that we don't want in our repository and prevent accidentally committing files we shouldn't.

```
$ dotnet new gitignore
```

Your directory becomes a Git repository with

```
$ git init
```

To stage the code created by the template (and the .gitignore file) for commit and then to commit it all to a first repository snapshot, we use two commands:

```
$ git add .
git commit -m "Create solution without test to later add
testing"
```

At this point, you have a clean working directory and *git status* will reflect this.

```
$ git status
branch main
nothing to commit, working tree clean
```

This means you're ready to add your .NET Aspire integration test project. To stay consistent with the way the rest of the projects in the solution are named, I'll follow the same convention of prefixing the project name with the solution name.

```
$ dotnet new aspire-xunit -n plain-starter-to-add-test.Tests
The template ".NET Aspire Test Project (xUnit)" was created
successfully.
This template contains technologies from parties other than
Microsoft, see https://aka.ms/dotnet/aspire/third-party-notices
for details.

Processing post-creation actions...
Restoring /home/raelyard/code/play/aspire-book-code/plain-
starter-to-add-test/plain-starter-to-add-test.Tests/plain-
starter-to-add-test.Tests.csproj:
Restore succeeded.
```

Before going any further, make sure to add your new project to your solution.

```
$ dotnet sln add plain-starter-to-add-test.Tests
Project `plain-starter-to-add-test.Tests/plain-starter-to-add-
test.Tests.csproj` added to the solution.
```

This is a good point to create a commit to have a new snapshot of the code in the Git repository.

```
$ git add .
git commit -m "Add project for integration tests"
[main 2d1d204] Add project for integration tests
 3 files changed, 71 insertions(+), 1 deletion(-)
 create mode 100644 plain-starter-to-add-test.Tests/
IntegrationTest1.cs
 create mode 100644 plain-starter-to-add-test.Tests/plain-
starter-to-add-test.Tests.csproj
```

The content of the project file generated this way is similar to the one created by the starter template with the test framework option, with one omission.

```
<Project Sdk="Microsoft.NET.Sdk">
  <PropertyGroup>
    <TargetFramework>net9.0</TargetFramework>
    <ImplicitUsings>enable</ImplicitUsings>
    <Nullable>enable</Nullable>
    <IsPackable>false</IsPackable>
    <IsTestProject>true</IsTestProject>
  </PropertyGroup>

  <ItemGroup>
    <PackageReference Include="Aspire.Hosting.Testing"
    Version="9.0.0" />
    <PackageReference Include="coverlet.collector"
    Version="6.0.2" />
    <PackageReference Include="Microsoft.NET.Test.Sdk"
    Version="17.10.0" />
    <PackageReference Include="xunit" Version="2.9.2" />
    <PackageReference Include="xunit.runner.visualstudio"
    Version="2.8.2" />
  </ItemGroup>

  <ItemGroup>
    <Using Include="System.Net" />
    <Using Include="Microsoft.Extensions.DependencyInjection" />
    <Using Include="Aspire.Hosting.ApplicationModel" />
    <Using Include="Aspire.Hosting.Testing" />
    <Using Include="Xunit" />
  </ItemGroup>

</Project>
```

The difference here is that the template for creating just a test project (and it works the same if you choose NUnit or MSTest – the test framework doesn't matter in this respect) does not add a reference to the AppHost project like it does with the starter solution template. If you think about it, this makes sense. When you create a new solution from the template, the designers of the template know about the AppHost project included in the template and it's straightforward to include a reference to it in the test project also generated at the same time. In the case of creating a new test project individually, there's no knowledge in the instantiation of the code of the broader context of what projects might already exist in the solution to which it is being added (or if it's even being added to an existing solution).

For this reason, adding a reference to the AppHost project in this scenario is your responsibility. It's straightforward to do so, so I'll go ahead and do it.

```
$ dotnet add plain-starter-to-add-test.Tests reference plain-
starter-to-add-test.AppHost
$ git commit -m "Create solution without test to later add
testing"
Reference `..\plain-starter-to-add-test.AppHost\plain-starter-
to-add-test.AppHost.csproj` added to the project.
```

Now, the project file has the necessary project reference that includes the generated code that makes it simple to run your distributed application from your testing process.

```
<Project Sdk="Microsoft.NET.Sdk">

  <PropertyGroup>
    <TargetFramework>net9.0</TargetFramework>
    <ImplicitUsings>enable</ImplicitUsings>
    <Nullable>enable</Nullable>
    <IsPackable>false</IsPackable>
```

```
  <IsTestProject>true</IsTestProject>
</PropertyGroup>

<ItemGroup>
  <PackageReference Include="Aspire.Hosting.Testing"
  Version="9.0.0" />
  <PackageReference Include="coverlet.collector"
  Version="6.0.2" />
  <PackageReference Include="Microsoft.NET.Test.Sdk"
  Version="17.10.0" />
  <PackageReference Include="xunit" Version="2.9.2" />
  <PackageReference Include="xunit.runner.visualstudio"
  Version="2.8.2" />
</ItemGroup>

<ItemGroup>
  <Using Include="System.Net" />
  <Using Include="Microsoft.Extensions.DependencyInjection" />
  <Using Include="Aspire.Hosting.ApplicationModel" />
  <Using Include="Aspire.Hosting.Testing" />
  <Using Include="Xunit" />
</ItemGroup>

<ItemGroup>
  <ProjectReference Include="..\plain-starter-to-add-test.
  AppHost\plain-starter-to-add-test.AppHost.csproj" />
</ItemGroup>

</Project>
```

The order of the elements might be a little different, but this is functionally the same project file as that created by using the solution template with the option for creating the test project. So, we've now added a project for integration tests with xUnit to an existing .NET Aspire solution.

This is another good time to create a source code snapshot via *git commit* in our repository with *git commit*.

```
$ git add .
$ git commit -m "Reference AppHost to enable integration
testing"
```

We're not done yet with getting to the point of having a working integration test. Really, the generated test that was created using the starter solution template in our earlier example was only an example of being able to make a request against a component of our distributed system. In this project, we have a similar generation of the test class, but it's less complete and not working right out of the box. Let's look at what got generated in *plain-starter-to-add-test.Tests/IntegrationTest1.cs*:

```
namespace plain_starter_to_add_test.Tests.Tests;

public class IntegrationTest1
{
    // Instructions:
    // 1. Add a project reference to the target AppHost
       project, e.g.:
    //
    //      <ItemGroup>
    //          <ProjectReference Include="../MyAspireApp.
               AppHost/MyAspireApp.AppHost.csproj" />
    //      </ItemGroup>
    //
    // 2. Uncomment the following example test and update
         'Projects.MyAspireApp_AppHost' to match your AppHost
         project:
```

```
//
// [Fact]
// public async Task GetWebResourceRootReturnsOk
   StatusCode()
// {
//     // Arrange
//     var appHost = await
       DistributedApplicationTestingBuilder.
       CreateAsync<Projects.MyAspireApp_AppHost>();
//     appHost.Services.ConfigureHttpClientDefaults
       (clientBuilder =>
//     {
//         clientBuilder.AddStandardResilienceHandler();
//     });
//     // To output logs to the xUnit.net
       ITestOutputHelper, consider adding a package from
       https://www.nuget.org/packages?q=xunit+logging
//
//     await using var app = await appHost.BuildAsync();
//     var resourceNotificationService = app.Services.
       GetRequiredService<ResourceNotificationService>();
//     await app.StartAsync();

//     // Act
//     var httpClient = app.CreateHttpClient("webf
       rontend");
//     await resourceNotificationService.WaitForResource
       Async("webfrontend", KnownResourceStates.Running).
       WaitAsync(TimeSpan.FromSeconds(30));
//     var response = await httpClient.GetAsync("/");
```

```
//      // Assert
//      Assert.Equal(HttpStatusCode.OK, response.
        StatusCode);
   // }
}
```

You'll notice immediately that all of the code in the test in this class is commented. Also, it's code embedded in a set of instructions offering a path to make a working test. Ultimately, you'll land on the same test as in the prior example if you follow these instructions. It's a sample test that checks the HTTP status code for a request to the root of your web application in your distributed application. This might be something you want if you have such a web application, but it's not the most useful of tests you can imagine. It does illustrate, though, the possibilities of being able to run your distributed application from your test suite, take actions against it (just like your users or integration partners would do), and make assertions on what you expect to result from those actions.

This form of testing is slower than unit testing, but it allows for powerful tests that make certain your system runs as a cohesive whole and that you get what you expect from running the whole system.

Summary

.NET Aspire does not change anything about the way you write unit tests for your code. You can continue to use your unit testing tools of choice and test your functions and other units as you always have. Aspire neither adds to nor subtracts from this. When you want to write broader tests, though, that run your whole system and interact with it in the ways your users and integrators do and assert that your system responds appropriately, .NET Aspire has support for that.

Using one of the project templates for testing with .NET Aspire includes package references that make it straightforward to run your system from your tests and to acquire client instances to interact with your system parts. This enables taking action against the system to arrange test conditions, act against the system in meaningful ways that test interactions, and assert that the results are what you expect.

The next chapter will cover .NET Aspire integrations that enable adding resources to your system and leverage them from your code. Integrations take care of a lot of the setup necessary for both hosting a particular type of resource and for consuming it. You'll get an introduction to the two types of packages that typically go together to make an integration and how they can help you improve your development experience.

CHAPTER 6

.NET Aspire Integrations

Modern cloud-native software development and deployment is driven largely by resources obtained from cloud providers and by containers (and often containers obtained for use in cloud provider environments). Cloud providers enable elastic provision and scale of a variety of types of resources, and containers enable packaging of software in more complete ways than was practically possible before. Like virtual machines, containers offer a way to create and ship runnable software with all the dependencies for running a given process, but with a fraction of the size and cost of creating the required images. This packaging of an environment and the portability provided by it has been game-changing in the ability to treat development and operations as sides of the same coin, instead of differing, and sometimes antagonistic, parts of an organization. The DevOps revolution owes a lot to the emergence of container technology.

In addition to repeatably and reliably deploying software to canonical environments, containers also have a story to tell for making the developer workstation experience better. Setting up a development environment can be done with the likes of Docker Compose to create dependency containers from images to serve the needs of running a system on a workstation.

© Dave Rael 2025
D. Rael, *Getting Started with .NET Aspire*, https://doi.org/10.1007/979-8-8688-1521-8_6

.NET Aspire goes a step further by introducing *integrations* to enable the use of cloud resources and containers to create runtime dependencies for systems, simply by running the orchestration mechanism built into .NET Aspire, the a*pp host* project. These integrations can create instances of a wide variety of resources that can take many forms. There are integrations that will create resources within a cloud provider. There are others that will use a container or containers to create resources. There are some that will create a cloud resource or a container depending on the way you set them up. Still others can host a runtime for platforms other than .NET. There aren't necessarily rules for what is allowed with integrations. They simply enable the inclusion of resources into your system, both in terms of hosting the integration and in consuming it.

You saw an introduction to integrations earlier when we used the *--use-redis-cache* option with the aspire-starter solution template to get a container workload running to serve as an ASP.NET Core output cache, using the Redis key-value store. You'll see more here about container technology itself as well as a much more complete treatment of what .NET Aspire integrations are, how to use them, and examples of what they can provide.

.NET Aspire and Aspire integrations are not only about containers. There is so much more to them than that. Still, containers are a big piece of the picture that enables a much more seamless experience with creating resources on a developer workstation. For this reason, I'll provide a brief introduction to what containers are and why they are useful before diving more fully into Aspire integrations.

Fundamentals: What Are Containers?

You've almost certainly come across containers if you've worked in modern information technology. It's an idea whose time has come and a significant advance to how software is done.

Even if you're familiar with using containers, though, it might be useful to dive briefly into what they really are and what they enable.

It's often said that containers can be thought of as lightweight virtual machines. This is not wrong, and it is a good approximation to what is really happening and is a useful way to think about the technology. So, as a first pass understanding, it's pretty good.

Containers do indeed behave like virtual machines with an isolated filesystem with its own set of permissions and boundaries and a process space that shares resources provided by the underlying host operating system with some controls on allocation of said resources to try to prevent containers from using resources in ways that impact other containers.

In all these ways, containers are, indeed, like virtual machines. Additionally, both virtual machine tools and container tools can be used to create images that can be used to repeatably create instances with characteristics defined by the image. It is this property that is useful in being able to create an image for a given version of a piece of software, along with all the dependencies it needs to run and just ship that image to create instances to run the software.

Containers differ from virtual machines in that with a virtual machine, the entire operating system is embedded into the image and therefore into the virtual machine instance itself. This makes for images and instances of relatively large sizes and that use resources in a way that is relatively heavy.

Containers, in contrast, don't require duplicating the whole operating system. Instead, they leverage the operating system kernel running on the host machine. The kernel is the core of the operating system that acts as the interface between the hardware and the software. This compromise means that containers require the kernel of the underlying operating system of the host to match what the container expects. In other words, Linux containers can only run on a Linux host.

In return for requiring this sameness of operating system, the container is freed from having to contain and run the operating system kernel, which means it's a lot smaller in size and requires fewer resources to run. Additionally, a virtual machine can serve as the host for containers such that one can run Linux containers on Windows host by having a host in the middle – a Linux virtual machine can run on a Windows or Mac host machine and in turn can host Linux containers as though the host machine were doing the hosting with a transparent experience for the user. This is how Docker Desktop works on both Windows and MacOS to create and run Linux container images and containers.

More fundamentally, containers were invented on top of the Linux kernel. The idea was to leverage some features of Linux to create an isolated process and filesystem space that could be treated as though it were an isolated machine.

This is far from the whole story, but Linux containers make use of features of the Linux filesystem and security system to treat an isolated space in the filesystem as though it were the root of a machine and to set user access and security properties to give an isolation for files and processes such that it appears to the user that shifting context to a container is shifting to something that behaves as though it were a different and isolated machine.

There is also such a thing as Windows containers. They generally work as a port of the ideas of Linux containers to running isolated spaces in Windows. It's the same idea but using a different implementation and with limitations and larger image sizes. Generally, as far as I'm aware, Windows containers are used when there are workloads that require Windows, such as running processes that will only work on Windows. Linux containers are usually preferred when they are an option. Additionally, Linux containers run on a wider variety of hosts and cloud platforms with much broader support. Generally, useful containers are mostly Linux containers. Popular container orchestration platforms, like Kubernetes, are centered on Linux containers. Fortunately, if you like Windows or MacOS, Docker Desktop makes it easy to use Linux containers on those platforms.

In short, containers are isolated process and filesystem spaces running on a machine with explicit security boundaries and tooling such that they appear to be, for most purposes, autonomous machines running within the host machine. Their light weight relative to virtual machines makes them even more portable and flexible for broad use. Treating container images as the deployable asset most suitable for reliable and repeatable shipping of quality software means shipping not just binaries, but runtime environments. When the deployable package includes the dependencies for running in the process, in addition to the process binaries, shipping becomes more repeatable and reliable.

Containers have been one of the biggest contributors to enabling modern software practices. In addition to making it easier to ship software within an organization, containers make it easier for an organization to share their software in ready-to-run packages via public container registries.

Having registries at our fingertips on the public Internet that make it easy to pull images and run containers from those images for most of the popular software and the building blocks for our systems makes this a great time to be alive and a great time to be a software developer.

What Is Docker and How Does It Relate to Containers?

Docker is the earliest and most popular toolset for working with containers. You can use containers without using Docker, but the ubiquity of Docker in the mindset of technology professionals makes it classically associated with container technology. For most technologists, when they think of containers, they think of Docker. Using Docker is straightforward and powerful, and it makes working with containers much easier than it would be without it.

Docker is composed of a runtime engine and client user interface tools, primarily the command-line client.

Installing Docker Desktop on Windows or Mac means you can let Docker manage creating the Linux virtual machines you need to run the Docker engine and just focus on building and using container images and containers. It also provides a graphical user interface in addition to *docker*, the command-line tool that communicates with the Docker engine.

Docker is free for personal use, but for businesses, professionals, and teams, there are licensing terms and prices that you need to consider. Always make sure you comply with the terms of the tools you use.

There are alternative toolsets to consider. .NET Aspire specifically supports Podman as an open source and free alternative. Most container examples you see, though, will use Docker as the tooling for working with containers, and it's generally advisable to use Docker unless you have reasons for using something else.

With .NET Aspire, you don't generally need to interact with Docker directly to take advantage of the containerized workloads you'll need. It's a good idea to be familiar with Docker and it will help with being able to troubleshoot and to operate more competently, but Aspire takes care of a lot of it for you.

There's a lot more that can be said about Docker and containers and building images, especially about leveraging the layered filesystem used in containers and making efficient use of the Docker build cache when you are building images, but with .NET Aspire integrations, our primary concern is with running containers and we'll let Aspire do that for us, so this is enough for now.

Introducing .NET Aspire Integrations

You don't need to be an expert on containers to use Aspire integrations. In fact, many of them won't use containers at all. A lot of them do, though. Knowing a little about containers is helpful, and to use integrations that do leverage containers, you'll need to have a container runtime installed. Other integrations might rely on having a language/platform runtime installed, like Python, Node.js, or Golang. Still others will need to have credentials for accessing an account in a cloud provider. You might need to consult documentation for any given integration to understand the requirements for running it.

If you have a container runtime installed on your workstation and you use the Redis caching option in the *aspire-starter* solution template, as we've already seen, running your app host leads to running your distributed system, which leads to having a resource of type *Container*.

When using the starter solution template, this was our first look at seeing what integrations are. Redis is only an example of a type of resource you might want to use in a distributed system. I'm sure you can think of several other examples in mere moments.

Integrations are generally published as a pair of library packages via NuGet. One of these libraries is for setting up the resource to run from your orchestrator, the a*pp host*. The other is for connecting your client processes to the resource via the dependency injection and service discovery made available by .NET and Aspire. The former of these libraries is known as the *hosting integration* and the latter as the *client integration.*

A hosting integration serves to enable adding a type of resource to your app model and is referenced by your app host project.

A client integration typically registers needed implementations with the dependency injection mechanism built into the ASP.NET Core into the processes you build to implement your system. In the example of the aspire-starter solution template, that means the ApiService and the Web projects. Most of the time, this means you'll reference the client integration in your project and call an extension method or some extension methods in your Program.cs for your process to register configured dependencies. The configuration of these implementations is set up with .NET Aspire service discovery. You'll then use them in your application code, resolved via dependency injection.

The way you'll use an integration will be easier to understand with examples.

You've already seen an example of using an integration in using Redis for caching in the solutions we've created earlier using the aspire-starter dotnet new solution template with the *–use-redis-cache* option. When we exercised that option, a reference was included in the app host project to the *Aspire.Hosting.Redis* package. This, with the inclusion of using an extension method from this package to create a container resource via calling *builder.AddRedis("cache")* in the app model, was the *hosting integration* side of using that integration. Instantiating the template with that option also included a reference to the *Aspire.StackExchange.Redis. OutputCaching* package in the Web project. This, with the inclusion of using an extension method from this package to wire up ASP.NET Core output caching, using the Redis instance running in our system, was the client integration side of using that integration. Taking this approach enabled the Web project to turn on output caching and find the running Redis container via service discovery by simply adding a call to *builder. AddRedisOutputCache("cache")* in the startup of the Web project.

This example is relatively simple and illustrates the power of .NET Aspire to make the developer workstation experience just work without fuss. Most of the integrations you'll use work like this. There's one, though, that has a lot more to think about and some rough edges you'll want to be aware of.

An Example of an Integration – SQL Server

The most common type of resource .NET developers will include in their systems is a relational database using SQL Server. There are, of course, other types of databases and other providers and brands of relational databases, but .NET and SQL Server go together frequently, so we should look at using the SQL Server integration and will use that as an example. Also, some of how the SQL Server integration works might surprise you, so it's good to get familiar with it.

If I want my distributed system to include SQL Server, I'll start with adding a reference to the .NET Aspire SQL Server hosting integration NuGet package to my app host project.

To get started quickly with having a solution with an app host project, as before, we can create a new solution from the command line with *dotnet new*.

```
$ dotnet new aspire-starter -o Demo.Sql
The template ".NET Aspire Starter App" was created
successfully.
This template contains technologies from parties other than
Microsoft, see https://aka.ms/dotnet/aspire/third-party-notices
for details.

Processing post-creation actions...
Restoring /home/raelyard/code/aspire-book-code/plain-starter-
to-add-sql/plain-starter-to-add-sql.sln:
Restore succeeded.
Restoring /home/raelyard/code/aspire-book-code/plain-starter-
to-add-sql/plain-starter-to-add-sql.AppHost/plain-starter-to-
add-sql.AppHost.csproj:
Restore succeeded.
Restoring /home/raelyard/code/aspire-book-code/plain-starter-
to-add-sql/plain-starter-to-add-sql.ServiceDefaults/plain-
starter-to-add-sql.ServiceDefaults.csproj:
Restore succeeded.
Restoring /home/raelyard/code/aspire-book-code/plain-starter-
to-add-sql/plain-starter-to-add-sql.ApiService/plain-starter-
to-add-sql.ApiService.csproj:
Restore succeeded.
```

```
Restoring /home/raelyard/code/aspire-book-code/plain-starter-
to-add-sql/plain-starter-to-add-sql.Web/plain-starter-to-add-
sql.Web.csproj:
Restore succeeded.
```

Now, change your directory context into the directory of the new solution.

```
$ cd Demo.Sql
```

You now have a solution, and you're ready to add your SQL Server hosting integration package to the app host project. The name of the package we'll use is *Aspire.Hosting.SqlServer*.

```
$ dotnet add Demo.Sql.AppHost package Aspire.Hosting.SqlServer
```

Now, to create a database server resource in your distributed application, open the *Program.cs* file in your app host project. Immediately before the creation of the apiService instance, add two lines of code. The first will add a database server to the system and the second will add a database.

```
var sqlServer = builder.AddSqlServer("sqlserver")
                .WithLifetime(ContainerLifetime.Persistent);
var database = sqlServer.AddDatabase("database");
```

The use of the *.WithLifetime()* call is something different from what we've seen so far with adding projects. It's not strictly necessary. In fact, depending on how you want to manage your test data, it may not be something you want at all. Setting a lifetime for a container resource is not specific only to SQL Server containers but applies to any container integration you might want to use.

In this case, *.WithLifetime()* with *ContainerLifetime.Persisent* means that when the app host shuts down, the container will not get destroyed. The default behavior is *ContainerLifetime.Session*, which leaves the container completely under the control of the app host. It starts when the app host starts and gets deleted when the app host stops. With a container lifetime set to *Persistent*, the app host, on starting, will try to find an existing container, and if it's already there, use it. If it's not there, it creates it. When the app host stops, it doesn't remove the container such that, for the next start, it will already be there. This means the system can start faster because of not having to create and run a new container. It also means that data in a database or something else with persistence in the container can survive from run to run.

This is not the whole story with persistent data, though. Experienced container users have probably already experienced that the filesystem in a container is ephemeral and lives with the container and goes away with it as well. For this reason, Docker and other container runtimes support volumes that can be mounted to container filesystems and that have different life cycles than the container itself.

The .NET Aspire hosting API also supports volumes and mounting them to containers, like SQL Server containers. Your purposes with the database you set up in a container may vary. In some cases, starting with a fresh database is exactly what you want for testing purposes, especially with automated tests. At other times, you might want an environment on your workstation that survives different runs and restarts of your machine. You are at liberty to run as you see fit.

There are some gotchas with the Aspire SQL Server integration. This will probably get better with time, but there are some things that don't work quite as you might expect.

First, making a call to add an SQL Server (*builder.AddSqlServer()*) to your app model does what you expect when running the app host and creates a server in a container. However, adding a database to that server does not create the database when you run the orchestration. This violation of expectation takes most developers by surprise. It turns out you need to do more with the SQL Server integration to make it work the way you expect, at least as of the time of writing. Adding a database to the model is adding a reference to it, not actually causing the creation of it.

Also, if you do want to use a persistent volume on your machine for a database server, you need to know that building a database server without giving it a password for the default administrator account causes one to be generated. Running the app host, stopping it, and then running again can cause a new database server container to be created (depending on the lifetime of the container, but even with a persistent container, there are other reasons it might get destroyed). A new database server container will create a new password if you're not explicit, and it will not be the same from run to run. With persistent data in a volume that a new container is trying to use with a different password than what's on disk in the volume, it won't work. For this reason, if you want to use a volume with SQL Server, you'll also want to be explicit with the password. Fortunately, this is supported. The *.AddSqlServer()* method has overloads that take additional parameters, including one that can take a password using a resource type known as a parameter.

Parameters are an Aspire resource type that can be created in your app model by calling the *IDistributedApplicationBuilder.AddParameter()* method. They enable setting up some configuration in your app host that can be made available to the broader system and/or to the dependencies you'll set up that aren't your system code.

It's a good idea if you want your developer workstation environment to include a database server using SQL Server that will survive restarts, to use a data volume and a password parameter. Using a parameter for a password means you should indicate that it's a secret value, such that publishing tools for .NET Aspire will be informed that the value should be treated with care and protected. These changes will mean the earlier code for adding your SQL Server and database will now look like

```
var saPassword = builder.AddParameter("sqlserverpassword",
secret: true);

var sqlServer = builder.AddSqlServer("sqlserver", saPassword)
    .WithLifetime(ContainerLifetime.Persistent)
    .WithDataVolume();
var database = sqlServer.AddDatabase("database");
```

Using a parameter in this way requires giving a value for the parameter in the app host configuration. This can be done on a developer machine using the likes of user secrets, or if the secret is not worth protecting for the data in use for development, it can just go into the appsettings.json file in the app host project. The latter is what I'll do for this demonstration to avoid additional complication. To make my password available, my appsettings.json will now become

```
{
  "Logging": {
    "LogLevel": {
      "Default": "Information",
      "Microsoft.AspNetCore": "Warning",
      "Aspire.Hosting.Dcp": "Warning"
    }
  },
  "Parameters": {
    "sqlserverpassword": "Super#!Secr3tPassw00rd"
  }
}
```

Now, running the app host, we can view the dashboard and see that this app model results in the two project resources we've seen before, but now there's a container resource that is our SQL Server and a new SqlServerDatabaseResource resource representing our database.

As mentioned before, this resource represents the database, but it doesn't create a database when we run the system. At this point, with having not specified a database name on the resource we added, this database resource refers to the default SQL database on the server, the *master* database. This means we wouldn't really need to create the database because it does already exist. This is almost certainly not what we want, though, for our system purposes. We'll want our application processes to connect to and use databases we created specifically to serve the needs of our users. As it is, with the database reference we have, we could start including references to the client integration for SQL Server to our application processes, but let's first change the overload we're using for *AddDatabase()* such that not only will we give the resource a name, but also a name for the database.

To the end of naming our database, we'll just add an extra parameter to the call to *AddDatabase()* with this parameter in the second position representing name of the database to which we should connect on the server.

```
var database = sqlServer.AddDatabase("database", "Weather");
```

Now, the database resource will reference that we want to connect to a database named "Weather" to serve the weather forecast summaries we're using in the sample API. We're going to be disappointed when we try to run this because we haven't set up anything yet to create such a database on the database server, but I'll say more on that later. For now, let's make our *apiservice* resource aware of the database by adding a call to *WithReference()* on the resource for our API in the app model to set up the connection for service discovery to make the database accessible to the running API process. This will make the whole of the Program.cs file in the app host project look like this:

```
var builder = DistributedApplication.CreateBuilder(args);

var saPassword = builder.AddParameter("sqlserverpassword",
secret: true);

var sqlServer = builder.AddSqlServer("sqlserver", saPassword)
    .WithLifetime(ContainerLifetime.Persistent)
    .WithDataVolume();

var database = sqlServer.AddDatabase("database", "Weather");

var apiService = builder.AddProject<Projects.Demo_Sql_
ApiService>("apiservice")
    .WithReference(database)
    .WaitFor(database);

builder.AddProject<Projects.Demo_Sql_Web>("webfrontend")
    .WithExternalHttpEndpoints()
    .WithReference(apiService)
    .WaitFor(apiService);

builder.Build().Run();
```

Now, we're ready to move from the hosting integration to the client integration. As mentioned, we'll need to return to the app host to make sure the database gets created, but let's look at the client integration now. To use the database in the ApiService project, we'll need to add a reference there to the client integration library, *Aspire.Microsoft.Data.SqlClient*.

```
$ dotnet add Demo.Sql.ApiService package Aspire.Microsoft.Data.
SqlClient
```

This package provides the extension method *IHostApplicationBuilder. AddSqlServerClient()* that we can use to register connections to an SQL database according to the name we gave it in the app model, and the connection string will just be provided by the service discovery built into .NET Aspire. This means that in the *Program.cs* in the ApiService project, we'll want to add, after the creation of the builder and before it gets built, the following line:

```
builder.AddSqlServerClient("database");
```

This will make the start of the file look like

```
var builder = WebApplication.CreateBuilder(args);

// Add service defaults & Aspire client integrations.
builder.AddServiceDefaults();

// Add services to the container.
builder.Services.AddProblemDetails();

// Learn more about configuring OpenAPI at https://aka.ms/
aspnet/openapi
builder.Services.AddOpenApi();

builder.AddSqlServerClient("database");

var app = builder.Build();
```

To very quickly just add a usage to the database, I'll just replace the hardcoded set of weather summaries

```
string[] summaries = ["Freezing", "Bracing", "Chilly", "Cool",
"Mild", "Warm", "Balmy", "Hot", "Sweltering", "Scorching"];
```

with a loop over the results of a database query using ADO.NET (against a table that does not exist in a database that does not exist). Typically, you wouldn't resolve database connection for application data purposes on starting the application, but for a simple example of accessing data, I'll resolve a connection explicitly from a scope, rather than using something like a controller where I'd be creating a database session in the scope of an API request or something of the sort.

```
List<string> summaries = [];

using (var scope = app.Services.CreateScope())
{
    using var connection = scope
        .ServiceProvider.GetRequiredService<SqlConnection>();
    var comamnd = connection.CreateCommand();
    comamnd.CommandText = "SELECT summary FROM Summaries";
    connection.Open();
    using var reader = comamnd.ExecuteReader();
    while (reader.Read())
    {
        summaries.Add(reader.GetString(0));
    }
}
```

This will require a *using* statement and a change of using the *Length* property of the array to the Count property of the *List* in the use of the collection.

```
using Microsoft.Data.SqlClient;
```

This makes the whole of the Program.cs file in the ApiService project look like this:

```
using Microsoft.Data.SqlClient;

var builder = WebApplication.CreateBuilder(args);

// Add service defaults & Aspire client integrations.
builder.AddServiceDefaults();
```

```
// Add services to the container.
builder.Services.AddProblemDetails();

// Learn more about configuring OpenAPI at https://aka.ms/
aspnet/openapi
builder.Services.AddOpenApi();

builder.AddSqlServerClient("database");

var app = builder.Build();

// Configure the HTTP request pipeline.
app.UseExceptionHandler();

if (app.Environment.IsDevelopment())
{
    app.MapOpenApi();
}

List<string> summaries = [];

using (var scope = app.Services.CreateScope())
{
    using var connection = scope.ServiceProvider.GetRequiredSer
vice<SqlConnection>();
    var comamnd = connection.CreateCommand();
    comamnd.CommandText = "SELECT summary FROM Summaries";
    connection.Open();
    using var reader = comamnd.ExecuteReader();
    while (reader.Read())
    {
        summaries.Add(reader.GetString(0));
    }
}
```

```
app.MapGet("/weatherforecast", () =>
{
    var forecast = Enumerable.Range(1, 5).Select(index =>
        new WeatherForecast
        (
            DateOnly.FromDateTime(DateTime.Now.AddDays(index)),
            Random.Shared.Next(-20, 55),
            summaries[Random.Shared.Next(summaries.Count)]
        ))
        .ToArray();
    return forecast;
})
.WithName("GetWeatherForecast");

app.MapDefaultEndpoints();

app.Run();

record WeatherForecast(DateOnly Date, int TemperatureC, string?
Summary)
{
    public int TemperatureF => 32 + (int)(TemperatureC
    / 0.5556);
}
```

If you run the app host with this code at this point, you'll see the attempt in the startup of the ApiService project to fail to connect to the database. This is because there is not a database on the server with the name "Weather." You shouldn't take my word for it – try it for yourself to see it fail. It's an exercise worth doing.

There is more than one way to resolve the problem of the database that does not exist. The ApiService code could check for existence of the database and create it if it doesn't already exist. I don't like doing this in proper application code, though, because it's a concern of setting up infrastructure and it's something that should happen on setup in anything except on a developer workstation. Code that should run only on a developer workstation is probably better left out of the code you'll ship to production.

For this reason, I find the code given by the Aspire team in a repository on GitHub giving samples to be greatly appealing. Instead of putting code into a project serving the business problem at hand, this sample code leverages the initialization of the SQL Server container to ensure the existence of the necessary database(s). This can also be used to create schemata, tables, seed data, and other resources to make the system work.

That samples repository can be found here: `https://github.com/dotnet/aspire-samples/`. Specifically, within that set of samples, there is an example of using database containers that includes not only SQL Server but also examples of using PostgreSQL and MySQL as well. The path to that example is `https://github.com/dotnet/aspire-samples/tree/main/samples/DatabaseContainers`.

Of particular interest is the way this sample leverages the entry point of the SQL Server container image to inject a customization of the startup script that starts the database server process when a container based on the image starts. By replacing the built-in entry point script, additional shell scripting is used to execute SQL scripts contained within a directory and the Aspire app model uses bind mounts to the container to put those scripts into a directory where they'll be executed.

This is relatively advanced stuff relating to running containers and overriding how they start. If you don't understand all of what's going on here, that's okay. The sample on GitHub has all the code you need to make this work.

It's a method of setting up a local database server that works smoothly, assuming you mount your files in the right places and the shell scripts have execute permission enabled.

Taking the SQL Server Example Further – Database Initialization

Because SQL Server is so commonly used among .NET developers and because the experience of using this integration is harder than most others, I'll continue this example by following the example from the samples repository and pointing out some places you could slip with it. It's really the best way I can think of to start with a working database in a system using Aspire but is more complicated than I'd like it to be.

Following the example set in this sample repository, to get my database integration to come up and give me not only a local SQL Server, but also a database dedicated to serving my ApiService project, I'll add a few files to my app host project and a little more code to the database server resource in my app model.

First, I'll create two subdirectories in my app host project directory – one for scripts to run on container entry and another for SQL scripts to be invoked by the shell scripts that will run on startup.

```
$ mkdir Demo.Sql.AppHost/sqlserverconfig
$ mkdir Demo.Sql.AppHost/sqlscripts
```

In the *sqlserverconfig* directory, I'll want to create two files. I'll name one of them entrypoint.sh and it will have the following content. This is something I took from the Aspire samples repository and didn't write myself.

```
#!/bin/bash

# Adapted from: https://github.com/microsoft/mssql-docker/
blob/80e2a51d0eb1693f2de014fb26d4a414f5a5add5/linux/preview/
examples/mssql-customize/entrypoint.sh

# Start the script to create the DB and user
/usr/config/configure-db.sh &
```

```
# Start SQL Server
/opt/mssql/bin/sqlservr
```

Notice that there's a comment in this file calling out the original source from which it was derived. That source script is the entrypoint.sh script that is built into the SQL Server container images published by Microsoft. This modification just injects calling another script – a script we'll also mount into our container.

That brings me to the second script we'll want to put in the *sqlserverconfig* directory. We'll name it *configure-db.sh*, and it will have the following content. Both of these scripts were sourced from the samples repository. The context for running both of these scripts is not directly on your machine, but in the container that serves as your SQL Server. This means you don't have to worry about these being bash scripts if you're running in a context without bash available. It will work because it's running in a container where it is available. What's happening in these scripts may not be obvious to .NET developers that have spent most of their time in Windows. If that's the case, don't worry. You just want to include these scripts in your app host project so they can be included in the container that is your database server. The net result of these two scripts is that the first one will execute at the start of the SQL Server container and it does what normally happens with SQL Server and also calls the second script. The second script, when called in this way, will execute all of the SQL scripts it finds in a given directory that we'll also include in the container. We'll use that directory to include a script to set up and seed our database.

```
#!/bin/bash

# set -x

# Adapted from: https://github.com/microsoft/mssql-docker/
blob/80e2a51d0eb1693f2de014fb26d4a414f5a5add5/linux/preview/
examples/mssql-customize/configure-db.sh
```

```
# Wait 120 seconds for SQL Server to start up by ensuring that
# calling SQLCMD does not return an error code, which will
ensure that sqlcmd is accessible
# and that system and user databases return "0" which means all
databases are in an "online" state
# https://docs.microsoft.com/sql/relational-databases/system-
catalog-views/sys-databases-transact-sql?view=sql-server-2017

dbstatus=1
errcode=1
start_time=$SECONDS
end_by=$((start_time + 120))

echo "Starting check for SQL Server start-up at $start_time,
will end at $end_by"

while [[ $SECONDS -lt $end_by && ( $errcode -ne 0 || ( -z
"$dbstatus" || $dbstatus -ne 0 ) ) ]]; do
    dbstatus="$(/opt/mssql-tools/bin/sqlcmd -h -1 -t 1 -U sa
    -P "$MSSQL_SA_PASSWORD" -C -Q "SET NOCOUNT ON; Select
    SUM(state) from sys.databases")"
    errcode=$?
    sleep 1
done

elapsed_time=$((SECONDS - start_time))
echo "Stopped checking for SQL Server
start-up after $elapsed_time seconds
(dbstatus=$dbstatus,errcode=$errcode,seconds=$SECONDS)"

if [[ $dbstatus -ne 0 ]] || [[ $errcode -ne 0 ]]; then
    echo "SQL Server took more than 120 seconds to start up or
    one or more databases are not in an ONLINE state"
    echo "dbstatus = $dbstatus"
```

```
    echo "errcode = $errcode"
    exit 1
fi

# Loop through the .sql files in the /docker-entrypoint-
initdb.d and execute them with sqlcmd
for f in /docker-entrypoint-initdb.d/*.sql
do
    echo "Processing $f file..."
    /opt/mssql-tools/bin/sqlcmd -S localhost -U sa -P "$MSSQL_
    SA_PASSWORD" -C -d master -i "$f"
done
```

If you're running on Linux or Mac, both script files will need to have execute permissions set on both script files. Windows users shouldn't have to do this because these permissions don't apply there, and it should just work even though these files are being executed in a Linux container. I have tried this, and it worked without having to do anything from PowerShell or cmd. If you are using Windows Subsystem for Linux (WSL), you're really using Linux and will need to set execute permissions. From Mac or Linux (including WSL), you'll want to execute these commands.

```
$ chmod +x Demo.Sql.AppHost/sqlserverconfig/entrypoint.sh
$ chmod +x Demo.Sql.AppHost/sqlserverconfig/configure-db.sh
```

It's important to do this because if you don't, the SQL Server container will fail on startup because it's unable to execute the scripts.

In addition to adding these shell script files, we'll also add an SQL file to the *sqlscripts* subdirectory of the app host project directory. The shell scripts included above will ensure that all SQL files in the directory where we'll mount this will get executed on our database server. I'll call this one ensuredatabase.sql and give it this content:

```sql
IF NOT EXISTS (SELECT * FROM sys.databases WHERE name =
N'Weather')
BEGIN
  CREATE DATABASE Weather;
END;
GO

USE Weather;
GO

IF NOT EXISTS (SELECT 1 FROM information_schema.tables WHERE
table_name = 'Summaries')
BEGIN
    CREATE table Summaries
    (
        Id int identity(1,1) primary key,
        Summary nvarchar(255) not null
    );
END;
IF NOT EXISTS (SELECT Summary FROM Summaries)
BEGIN
    insert Summaries (Summary) values ('Freezing');
    insert Summaries (Summary) values ('Bracing');
    insert Summaries (Summary) values ('Chilly');
    insert Summaries (Summary) values ('Cool');
    insert Summaries (Summary) values ('Mild');
    insert Summaries (Summary) values ('Warm');
    insert Summaries (Summary) values ('Balmy');
    insert Summaries (Summary) values ('Hot');
    insert Summaries (Summary) values ('Sweltering');
    insert Summaries (Summary) values ('Scorching');
END;
```

This script will check if a database named *Weather* exists. If it does, it will continue without taking action, and if it doesn't, it will create it. It will then move into a context of using the *Weather* database that now certainly exists. It will then check if a table named *Summaries* exists. If it does, it will continue without taking action, and if it doesn't, it will create it. It will then check if there are rows in the Summaries table that now certainly exists. If there are, it will finish without taking any further action. If there aren't any rows, it will insert rows matching the static array that was generated in the hardcoded form of the ApiService project code. The net result is that we'll start our system with the database we need, the table (singular in this simple example) we need, and seed data to make our system work.

With these files in place, let's return to our app model (the Program.cs file in the app host project). Recall that, before, we were setting up our SQL Server with this code:

```
var sqlServer = builder.AddSqlServer("sqlserver", saPassword)
    .WithLifetime(ContainerLifetime.Persistent)
    .WithDataVolume();
```

Now, to leverage the new entrypoint.sh script we've created, we'll change that to

```
var sqlServer = builder.AddSqlServer("sqlserver", saPassword)
    .WithBindMount("./sqlserverconfig", "/usr/config")
    .WithBindMount("./sqlscripts", "/docker-entrypoint-initdb.d")
    .WithEntrypoint("/usr/config/entrypoint.sh")
    .WithLifetime(ContainerLifetime.Persistent)
    .WithDataVolume();
```

To understand what this code is now doing, first look at the creation of the two bind mounts we've added. Using a bind mount in a container is essentially a mapping of a directory on disk on your host machine to a path on the filesystem of the container. The first bind mount here is taking the sqlserverconfig subdirectory of the app host directory and mounting it to the path */usr/config* in the SQL Server container. This makes the files we created available to the container at runtime. The second bind mount is taking the *sqlscripts* subdirectory of the app host project directory and making it available in the container at the path */docker-entrypoint-initdb.d*.

Finally, the line calling the *WithEntrypoint()* method is saying that the container runtime should start up the process that runs inside the running container with the script at the path */usr/config/entrypoint.sh*, which is where we've just mounted out custom entrypoint script.

The net result of all of this is that when the SQL Server starts, it will run every SQL file in the sqlscripts subdirectory of the app host project on our workstation disk. This is an extremely useful pattern, not only for this demonstration, but for your systems as well.

Now, if you run the app host project, you should have all resources up and running and you should be able to observe that the ApiService project now successfully queries the database on startup and serves results accordingly. In a real application process, you probably wouldn't have a single query at startup, but this is a simple example of interacting with a database via the service discovery made available by creating references in the app model in our app host project.

More on SQL Server

In the example of the previous section, I showed you using a hosting integration and client integration to work with SQL Server. Those packages are not the whole story.

Object-relational mappers are useful tools and Microsoft's Entity Framework Core is extremely popular, not only because it's a powerful way to bridge the impedance mismatch between the object and relational worlds but also because of top-notch support for database migrations, enabling versioning of database schema and more.

If you want to use Entity Framework Core, there's an integration for that. It's documented here: `https://learn.microsoft.com/dotnet/aspire/database/sql-server-entity-framework-integration`. You'll likely want to use the same hosting integration when using when using Entity Framework. On the hosting side, you're just enlisting an instance of SQL Server into your app model. On the client side, though, you'll want to use a different client integration package. In this case, you'd reference *Aspire.Microsoft.EntityFrameworkCore.SqlServer* instead of *Aspire.Microsoft.Data.SqlClient.* In the Program.cs in your consuming process, the extension method you'll use to register your DBContext is *IHostApplicationBuilder.AddSqlServerDbContext<T>(),* where T is the type of your context, derived from DbContext. If you're not familiar with Entity Framework Core, the DbContext is the root type you'll use to interact with your data using collection semantics (this is known as the repository pattern). This contrasts with registering *SqlConnection* with the SqlClient client integration. The workings are similar, though. With this call when your application starts up, you'll be able to resolve a context and work with your database, this time using an Entity Framework context instead of SqlConnection, SqlCommand, and friends.

There are some other options for hosting integrations for SQL Server, too. Generally, the problem .NET Aspire solves is making your life easier in running systems on your developer workstation. That often means you want to run a local SQL Server for database needs (and/or local instances of whatever other dependencies you may take on). This makes your development and testing faster than using networked resources, enables disconnected work, and is usually more stable. Running completely locally is not the only way, though. There are reasons you might want to use a database in the cloud for your development work.

In addition to the developer experience, you'll want to put some thought into the deployment of your systems. In the next chapter, you're going to see some examples of deployment of .NET Aspire systems. One of the most straightforward ways to deploy with Aspire is to use the Azure

Developer command-line interface to deploy to Azure Container Apps, which is a serverless part of the Azure cloud offering that runs workloads in containers.

The automatic deployment of an Aspire system to Azure Container Apps is useful for demonstration purposes. For deployments to canonical environments, you'll probably have a more formal process, though, involving pipelines and artifacts and promotion of environments. You may have some Infrastructure as Code work that provides resources such that just deploying to Azure Container Apps might not be enough.

Still, there are cases where such a deployment method might work for your organization, or there might be times you want to enable testing on something not yet ready to be integrated into your repository's main line.

If you were to take sample we built in the prior section, using the Aspire SQL Server integration, and deploy it with *azd*, the Azure Developer command-line tool, it would indeed create this system in Azure container apps. In the next chapter, we'll do this very thing, and you'll see the database server get created in a container in this system.

That's right – on deploying to Azure, with your application processes running in containers in Azure Container Apps, the resource that is the database server is yet another container in the Container Apps Environment that gets created.

This might surprise you. You might expect that deploying your system to Azure would create SQL Server resources using Azure SQL instead of creating a container from an SQL Server image to run in that environment.

The reason for this is that this integration is specifically implemented by running SQL Server in a container. It works to do this and you could run your database in a container this way in a real environment.

You'd likely, though, prefer to let Azure manage your SQL Server for you, by using Azure SQL. You can do this with using a different integration.

.NET Aspire provides numerous integrations serving many different types of resoucres. Another integration is one for Azure SQL. If, instead of having used the SQL Server integration, we had used the Azure SQL integration, the resulting database server would have defaulted to an Azure SQL Server. The Azure SQL hosting integration is in a package called *Aspire.Hosting.Azure.Sql*. The Azure SQL hosting integration, by default, when running on your workstation, will try to use Azure credentials stored on your machine to create a database for you in an Azure subscription. It can be instructed, though, to use a container locally.

You might envision scenarios where you would use a conditional on the environment in which you are running to determine whether you run in a database in Azure or call the *IDistributedApplicationBuilder. RunAsContainer()* extension method to keep your workstation environment self-contained.

You have a lot of options for how you run and how you might want to deploy your system to environments beyond your machine. In the next chapter, we'll look at some options for deployment, including seeing what happens when deploying a system that includes SQL Server into Azure with the Azure Developer command-line interface to get more exposure to what happens with an integration, especially the hosting integration for SQL Server.

Summary

.NET Aspire integrations are powerful NuGet packages that make it straightforward to include a variety of resources into your system. Some examples of resources provided by integrations are key-value datastores like Redis, message brokers like RabbitMQ, relational database like SQL Server, language/platform runtimes like Rust, and many others. Integrations often come in pairs of NuGet packages, one to host the integration and one to consume it, called the hosting integration and the client integration (though some have only a hosting integration package). Integrations give you a simple way of using resources in your system with support for customizing them to fit your needs.

So far, we've been primarily concerned with running systems on developer workstations. There's a good reason for this. The developer experience is the main driving force behind .NET Aspire. It does have more to offer, though. In the next chapter, we'll look at deployment of systems that use .NET Aspire and how Aspire can contribute.

CHAPTER 7

Deploying Your Aspire-Based System

Developing software and running it on your workstation is a good start to having a running system. Improving the developer experience of working with distributed systems, as .NET Aspire does, is a game-changing leap forward. That alone is not enough, though.

To make software truly useful, you need to make it available to end users, so they can realize the value provided by the running system. To do this, you need to deploy your software somewhere beyond your own workstation.

.NET Aspire solves a lot of the problems of working with a distributed system on your machine by making it easy to bring up multiple processes from .NET projects and other types of projects with other languages, as well as workloads in containers via integrations and standalone containers to make for a single starting point for a whole system. This is a win. It's not the end of the story, though.

Deploying your software to nonproduction environments for testing and, ultimately, to production environments to serve real users is essential to having a successful operation. .NET Aspire and some tools around it are helpful in making this straightforward, in addition to helping bridge the gap for the developer workstation.

© Dave Rael 2025
D. Rael, *Getting Started with .NET Aspire*, https://doi.org/10.1007/979-8-8688-1521-8_7

You have many choices for where you'll deploy your software. This overview will not cover every option. It will give you an idea, though, of the landscape and how to get started with getting working software delivered to make it truly valuable.

Options for Deploying Distributed Systems

It's not universally true that the days of on-premises deployments are gone, but the world is moving in that direction.

When I picture modern software systems, cloud providers are almost always in the picture. Even if you are in an organization with your own datacenter footprint and you (or coworkers) are managing hardware, you're likely using virtualization platforms or something that resembles cloud offerings by making compute, storage, and networking available via some sort of API or other systemic approach. It could be that you have built Kubernetes clusters using bare-metal machines as nodes. One way or another, chances are that even if you're not running in one of the popular cloud providers, you're using something cloud native or an approximation of it.

There are reasons for the modern dominance of cloud-native tools and platforms. They simplify the provision of resources relative to having to manage your own infrastructure and provide the ability to scale drastically and dramatically without having to deal with adding hardware and they allow what you spend to rise with your need, rather than having to statically provision for your largest load, leaving excess capacity at nonpeak times.

Without cloud platforms, we wouldn't have cloud-native toolsets and the notion of Infrastructure as Code would not be conceivable, at least, not in the ways we think about it today.

So, it's natural to think about deploying software in terms of how you'd do it in various cloud providers and/or using cloud-native tools that work, at least to an extent, in similar ways in different clouds. Further, .NET and .NET Aspire are Microsoft technologies, and they have a primary focus on working nicely with Microsoft Azure.

For these reasons, I'll look at deployment options for Aspire systems in Azure first. Also, you should be aware that there is support for integrating Amazon Web Services (AWS) with .NET Aspire in the form of a package called *Aspire.Hosting.AWS* that provides AppHost integration for using CloudFormation templates for hooking into your app model. Finally, because it has become ubiquitous in association with cloud-native deployment and container orchestration and is supported by just about every cloud provider out there (including the smaller players), I'll take you through deployment to Kubernetes clusters.

.NET Aspire and Azure – Collaboration of Siblings

It makes sense that an opinionated framework for creating distributed applications built by Microsoft would work nicely with Microsoft's cloud platform offering, Azure. It's also not surprising that Aspire has nice integration with tooling provided by Microsoft. This is true of using .NET Aspire with the .NET command-line interface and Visual Studio, as we have seen. It's also true of using .NET Aspire with a tool called the Azure Developer command-line interface (azd). This is a tool designed to quickly and easily create resources in Azure. It works from templates that can generate Bicep, a language used by Azure for creating resources. It also knows how to read a .NET Aspire orchestrator project and create a configuration that will deploy that project to Azure Container Apps. This is a very easy way to get your application out into the cloud and available for use. Azure Container Apps is a serverless platform that provides a security boundary in which you can run privately networked resources and only make available to the broader Internet what you choose. It's certainly useful for quick deployment and demonstration. It may or may not fit the needs of what you're really trying to do with your deployments to canonical environments and may or may not be the most cost-effective way to deploy, depending on a lot of factors and the nature of your organization. Even if it's not exactly what you want for your ultimate destination for production, it can be useful for some lesser environments, especially environments on demand, perhaps for testing of feature branch code before merging pull requests. There are a lot of possibilities for using this capability of deploying Aspire-based systems. Also, it's likely the Azure Developer CLI will provide other deployment options in the future.

One way or another, let's dive into what it's like to deploy to Azure Container Apps with the Azure Developer CLI. This is not the only way to deploy a system that uses Aspire to Azure, but it is the simplest and the fastest, so it's worth a look.

The first step is to install azd. This is straightforward and the documentation offers easy instructions, using WinGet on Windows, Homebrew on Mac, or a shell script or package manager on Linux. When installed, the executable is called *azd*. The installation instructions can be found at `https://learn.microsoft.com/azure/developer/azure-developer-cli/install-azd`.

Note   This tool is the Azure Developer command-line interface (azd), not the Azure command-line interface (az). Both exist and are useful tools. It might be easy to confuse the two. az is a tool for issuing commands from your terminal that directly invoke the Azure API. It's more of a low-level tool for doing things you might otherwise do directly with the Azure API or in the Azure portal. azd is a higher-level tool for the provision of resources and deployment of application processes to Azure as defined in templates and with configuration for potentially multiple environments. This book will not cover anything related to using the Azure command-line interface, but if you use Azure, it's something you'll want to be familiar with. The demonstration later in this chapter of deploying to Kubernetes will use a local cluster constructed from containers on your workstation, merely as an example. If, however, you want to interact with a cluster in Azure, you'll use Azure Kubernetes Service and will likely want to authenticate with it with az. Similarly, you'd use command-line tools from AWS, Google Cloud, Linode, Digital Ocean, or any other provider to authenticate and create contexts for clusters in those environments.

To set up a .NET Aspire system to deploy with azd, first set your terminal context to either the AppHost project directory or the root directory of your solution (this can be any .NET Aspire solution, so you can create a new one with the starter template or any other means or use one you've already created from prior samples). If you're in the solution directory, it will find your AppHost and detect that it's dealing with a .NET Aspire system.

For my demonstration, and to show a little of what you can do with Azure resources, I'll use the system I created in the prior chapter that used an integration for creating a database using Sql Server. We'll first see deployment create the database in my app model using a container in the container app and then modify it to use Azure Sql instead.

From my solution directory, with azd installed, I can get started with the *init* command. It can take parameters or get required information from environment variables named according to convention. Instead of specifying everything upfront, though, to get familiar with what it does for Aspire, I'll just issue the command and let it ask for the further input it needs. It will first ask how I want to proceed via a menu, and I'll choose the first and selected-by-default option of using code in the current directory by just keying *Enter* again.

Note   The output of azd may change between the time when this was written and when you are using it.

```
$ azd init

Initializing an app to run on Azure (azd init)

? How do you want to initialize your app?  [Use arrows to move,
type to filter]
> Use code in the current directory
  Select a template
  Create a minimal project
```

It will take a finite amount of time while showing a message saying it's scanning my code.

```
|==      | Scanning app code in current directory
```

When it finishes, it now tells me that it has detected .NET (Aspire) and will deploy on Azure using Azure Container Apps.

```
(✓) Done: Scanning app code in current directory

Detected services:

  .NET (Aspire)
  Detected in: /system/system.AppHost/system.AppHost.csproj

azd will generate the files necessary to host your app on Azure
using Azure Container Apps.

? Select an option  [Use arrows to move, type to filter]
> Confirm and continue initializing my app
  Cancel and exit
```

If I choose the default option from the menu "Confirm and continue initializing my app," it will ask me for an environment name. I'll just use *play* as my environment name.

```
? Enter a new environment name: [? for help]
```

The output at this point tells me it has completed and notes the files that have been created and some useful instructions for continuing.

Generating files to run your app on Azure:

```
(✓) Done: Generating ./azure.yaml
(✓) Done: Generating ./next-steps.md

SUCCESS: Your app is ready for the cloud!
```

In addition to having generated the two files mentioned in the output, it also generated a hidden subdirectory called *.azure* and modified my .gitignore file to exclude that hidden subdirectory. The contents of that subdirectory are specific to your setup and the environment you have created, so you'll not want to commit them to your repository. This is the reason for the addition to .gitignore. The markdown file, next-steps.md, offers some useful information. It wouldn't do any harm to commit it to your repository, but it's probably something you'll want to read and then delete. The information there is good. It points out that you can use azd to go ahead and deploy your system via the *azd up* command and that you can do discreet steps instead to first provision the cloud resources and then to deploy your built application processes if you prefer. Either way, the net result will be a deployed and working Azure Container Apps resource, along with supporting resources, in Azure for your .NET Aspire distributed system.

I'll go ahead and deploy in one step using *azd up*, but it won't work without another necessary step (if you're not already logged in to an Azure account with azd). Thus far, all the interactions I've had with azd have been purely local on my filesystem. That's because it has been all about analyzing my code and deciding how it would deploy my software to Azure if it was deploying it, but without actually doing any deployment. We're changing that now. If I tell azd any of *provision, deploy,* or *up* (up does both provision and deploy), it's going to need to interact with Azure and it's going to need to do it on my behalf. To do that, I'll need to log in. In fact, the output of *azd up* will tell me just that (and helpfully how to resolve the problem).

```
$ azd up

ERROR: not logged in, run `azd auth login` to login
```

After I log with *az auth login*, the story is different. Now, azd is able to talk to Azure in my logged in account and create the necessary resources for deploying my creation.

Note   If you have done what I have with the trick of using bind mounts in your app model in setting up your SQL Server to be able to run SQL on starting your server to create a database, schema, and see data, using bind mounts with Azure Container Apps via the Azure Develop command-line interface will only work if you set a prerelease option to enable it working. You can do that with

---

```
$ azd config set alpha.azd.operations on
```

Once you have set this option (or if you're deploying something that doesn't use bind mounts), you're ready to go ahead and deploy with the *up* command.

```
$ azd up
|    ===| Analyzing Aspire Application (this might take a
moment...)
```

You'll see changing output as azd goes through a few steps of analyzing your application and generating Bicep for deployment. Ultimately, it will ask you what subscription you want to use (which is only an interesting question if your Azure account has more than one subscription). After selecting the appropriate subscription, you'll be asked what Azure region you want to use. It will probably default to one close to you. If not, you should select one close to you and press *Enter* to continue.

It will take some time (minutes) for the deployment to complete. You'll see output in your terminal indicating progress and a link to the Azure portal to be able to see progress and creation of your resources in your browser as it proceeds.

```
(✓) Done: Upgrading Bicep
? Select an Azure Subscription to use:  1. Pay-As-You-Go Dev/
Test (xxxxxxxx-xxxx-xxxx-xxxx-xxxxxxxxxxxx)
? Select an Azure location to use: 44. (US) Central US
(centralus)

Packaging services (azd package)

Provisioning Azure resources (azd provision)
Provisioning Azure resources can take some time.

Subscription: xxx
Location: Central US

  You can view detailed progress in the Azure Portal:
https://portal.azure.com/#view/HubsExtension/
DeploymentDetailsBlade/~/overview/id/%2Fsubscriptions%2Fxxx
```

```
(✓) Done: Resource group: rg-play (1.644s)
(✓) Done: Container Registry: acrvwy3kj4fxd5ik (8.973s)
(✓) Done: Log Analytics workspace: law-vwy3kj4fxd5ik
    (16.821s)
|     ==| Creating/Updating resources (Container Apps
    Environment)
```

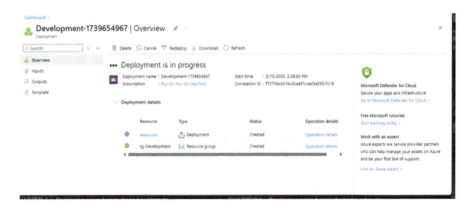

Figure 7-1. *Azure portal showing azd deployment to Azure Container Apps of a .NET Aspire system*

Ultimately, this is going to land on having a working system in Azure. At the conclusion of successful deployment, the output in my terminal looks like this:

```
(✓) Done: Resource group: rg-Development (1.111s)
(✓) Done: Container Registry: acrgjemyl5amx5hy (3.811s)
(✓) Done: Log Analytics workspace: law-gjemyl5amx5hy
    (17.297s)
(✓) Done: Container Apps Environment: cae-gjemyl5amx5hy
    (1m36.772s)

Deploying services (azd deploy)
```

```
(✓) Done: Deploying service apiservice
- Endpoint: https://apiservice.internal.
victoriousdesert-52f98e7b.centralus.azurecontainerapps.io/

(✓) Done: Deploying service cache
- Endpoint: https://cache.internal.victoriousdesert-52f98e7b.
centralus.azurecontainerapps.io/

(✓) Done: Deploying service webfrontend
- Endpoint: https://webfrontend.victoriousdesert-52f98e7b.
centralus.azurecontainerapps.io/

Aspire Dashboard: https://aspire-dashboard.ext.
victoriousdesert-52f98e7b.centralus.azurecontainerapps.io
```

```
SUCCESS: Your up workflow to provision and deploy to Azure
completed in 3 minutes 20 seconds.
```

This shows how easy it is, with the tight integration of .NET Aspire, Azure, and the Azure Developer CLI, to get a distributed system up and running in Azure. Your options for how to deploy are limited with this method, as deploying to an Azure Container Apps Environments is the only option. It would not be surprising, though, to see further development to make it more flexible with more options in the future.

Azure Container Apps is a sophisticated offering that makes it really easy to get running software in the cloud without having to make a lot of decisions. It's great for many use cases and is good for creating a personal environment to review and test changes before taking them to a broader audience. It's a production-ready way to run and can serve your long-lived canonical environments. It's also good for quick, temporary environments. Further personal projects you may take on might benefit from this ease of deployment and straightforward but powerful setup of an environment.

Having deployed this system to Azure, let's look at the resources created in the Azure portal.

Name ↑	Type ↑↓	Resource group ↑↓	Location ↑↓
acrvwy3kj4fxd5ik	Container registry	rg-play	Central US
apiservice	Container App	rg-play	Central US
cae-vwy3kj4fxd5ik	Container Apps Environment	rg-play	Central US
law-vwy3kj4fxd5ik	Log Analytics workspace	rg-play	Central US
mi-vwy3kj4fxd5ik	Managed Identity	rg-play	Central US
sqlserver	Container App	rg-play	Central US
volvwy3kj4fxd5ik	Storage account	rg-play	Central US
webfrontend	Container App	rg-play	Central US

Figure 7-2. *Azure portal showing resources resulting from a completed azd deployment to Azure Container Apps of a .NET Aspire system*

You'll notice that among the resources created, there's a container registry. This is an Azure resource that serves as a private registry for you to push images to and pull images from. The reason it was created by *azd*, in this case, is that it can push images to the registry in your subscription and then the Container Apps Environment can be populated with containers built from your images, sourced from the registry. This registry is private to your Azure subscription and nobody else can get to your images.

Notice, also, the resource that is the Container Apps Environment itself. This is a contained environment in which you can run your workloads in containers and the outside world can't get in unless you allow it. The Aspire projects we have created have created a Blazor web frontend project and call the *.WithExternalHttpEndpoints()* extension method on the resource in the app model. This call causes that container app to have public Internet exposure such that the web user interface can be reached without being in any sort of private network. The ApiService project resource does not have that call and is therefore available only within the Container Apps Environment and not externally.

Looking at the Container Apps Environment resource in the Azure portal reveals a few interesting pieces of information. For one, you can see that the portal got deployed and is available with a link that says, "Open dashboard." Sure enough, clicking through shows the dashboard with which we are familiar, running in this new environment in Azure.

Figure 7-3. .NET Aspire dashboard running in Azure Container Apps, resulting from an azd deployment of a .NET Aspire system

Clicking again in the dashboard to the webfrontend URL reveals our web application, as you might expect. Also, as expected, clicking the URL for the API does not successfully reach the API, which is not exposed publicly. Trying to request the URL for the ApiService project from my browser results in a not found page.

Figure 7-4. *Not Found error message page from Azure Container Apps when trying to request a resource not exposed to the outside Internet*

This API application endpoint is not reachable from the outside Internet but is available to the web frontend application. The networking needs for different use cases will vary, but it's encouraging to see that what you specify in your app model comes to life so precisely in this environment.

You can see that, in relatively short order, you're able to create a distributed system using .NET Aspire, run it quickly and easily on your workstation with easy access to useful telemetry, and then deploy it to an environment in the cloud, also quickly and easily. Without .NET Aspire, it would have been a lot more difficult and time-consuming to get to this point.

This is all under your control in the app model in your AppHost project and you can imagine the many ways you could extend this simple distributed system into something more useful and real for addressing real-world needs.

We've now created an environment in Azure to run our application. It was quick and simple. Tearing it down is just as easy. In the same way you used the *up* command to deploy your system, you can use the *down* command to tear it down.

```
$ azd down
```

This will ask for confirmation and then destroy your resources. This is important. Always remember that running workloads in the cloud comes at a cost and it can be unpleasant when you are surprised with an unexpectedly high bill. The simple systems we've created with these samples shouldn't cause great risk of breaking the bank, but you should always be conscious of what costs you are incurring, and they can add up quickly as you add more resources to your systems.

In the previous chapter, when talking about the SQL Server integration, I mentioned that deploying the system with that integration into Azure Container Apps would result in running SQL Server in a container in the Container Apps Environment. That's exactly what we observed here.

Among the resources shown in the Azure portal was a Container App called sqlserver. This is my database server, running in a container, similar to the experience I had on my workstation.

Integrating Azure SQL Instead

If, instead of using the *Aspire.Hosting.SqlServer* hosting integration package, you use the *Aspire.Hosting.Azure.Sql* hosting integration package and set up your app model accordingly, the result of deploying will reflect a different set of resources.

Instead of running SQL Server in a container app, you'll wind up with an Azure SQL Server and an Azure SQL database. Depending on what you want, this may be a more desirable result.

☐ 🔷 acrvwy3kj4fxd5ik	Container registry
☐ 🔷 apiservice	Container App
☐ 🔷 cae-vwy3kj4fxd5ik	Container Apps Environment
☐ 🔷 law-vwy3kj4fxd5ik	Log Analytics workspace
☐ 🔑 mi-vwy3kj4fxd5ik	Managed Identity
☐ 🔷 sqlserver-vwy3kj4fxd5ik	SQL server
☐ 🔷 weather (sqlserver-vwy3kj4fxd5ik/weather)	SQL database
☐ 🔷 webfrontend	Container App

Figure 7-5. *Azure portal showing resources resulting from a completed azd deployment to Azure Container Apps of a .NET Aspire system, including Azure SQL as opposed to SQL Server in a container*

Your needs for different environments may vary and you may have some desire for switching the types of resources you use, depending on the environment. You can do that with conditionals in your app model if you choose. You may also have environments where you set up resources with some sort of Infrastructure as Code, like Terraform, instead of letting the app model generate what you deploy. You'd then do your deployments via some other mechanism that you set up yourself.

In short, you have options. .NET Aspire is useful for delivering a stellar developer experience. It may also be helpful for deploying to some or all your environments. You have choices on all aspects of how your organization delivers software.

.NET Aspire and Kubernetes – Meet Aspir8

Kubernetes is a massive open-source project and community that grew out of efforts at Google to create a robust platform for scalable software. It has become the world's most popular and talked about platform for operating cloud-native software in containers. It's a powerful orchestrator with full consideration for scale, load balancing, fault tolerance, health monitoring, and more. It's supported just about anywhere you want to run your software, including all the major and minor cloud providers and on-premises.

It's widely supported and wisely used. It has vast communities of users and organizations putting it through every usage scenario you can imagine.

There is a community-supported open-source project dedicated to turning a .NET Aspire app model and turning it into container images in a registry and manifests for deploying to Kubernetes. It's called Aspir8, or Aspirate. It installs as a command-line tool and offers flexible options for building images and pushing them to a registry, in addition to generating manifests and configuration for running a system in a Docker Compose network or for deploying to Kubernetes.

Aspir8 is clearly useful if you want to deploy your system to Kubernetes. Even if you don't want to use Kubernetes, it's still a convenient tool for building container images from your projects if that's something you want to do.

It installs as a tool with the dotnet command-line interface and is most useful when installed globally.

Note   Because of the state of the project of active development as of the time of writing, the documentation recommends installing the latest version using the *–prerelease* option. That may change, so you'll want to look at the documentation.

The getting started documentation that describes installation is here: https://prom3theu5.github.io/aspirational-manifests/installing-as-a-global-tool.html. Installation is done with

```
$ dotnet tool install -g aspirate --prerelease
```

Note   On Windows, the dotnet global tools install path should be on your path by default, enabling you to just use the *aspirate* executable from anywhere on your filesystem. On Linux, especially, it's probably not there by default, and to be able to just use *aspirate* from your project path, you'll want to add it to your *PATH* environment variable. The global installation location for dotnet tools on Linux (and Mac) is *$HOME/.dotnet/tools* and that's what you'll want to add to your *PATH* to make it globally accessible. There's a note on this on the documentation for dotnet tools installation: `https://learn.microsoft.com/dotnet/core/tools/dotnet-tool-install#installation-locations`.

With Aspir8 installed globally (and your *PATH* properly including global dotnet tools), the executable, named aspirate, is now available. As with many tools, the first step in using it is to issue the *init* command. *aspirate init* will ask you a few questions that will help make it especially useful to your team. You are at liberty not to set these configurations, as there are some defaults. The answers you give (or don't give) to these questions will go into the configuration file generated by the *init* command.

The first question is whether you want to use a default container registry for your projects. It informs you that you can set registries on a project-by-project basis and that for any project that doesn't have a registry, this fallback value will be used. If you don't set a default and projects don't specify where to push your container images, it will just build images locally and not push them to a registry. If there is a registry specified in either place, Aspir8 will push an image it builds there.

It also asks if you'd like to set a repository prefix for the images you build. This is simply a prefix for the name of the image you're creating. The names of container images are called *repositories* because the name represents a common name for multiple images, usually different versions of the same application code, distinguishable by tags. This is something that often causes confusion. If you want the images in your system to have repositories (names) with a common prefix, this input to Aspir8 will accomplish that.

The main output of *aspirate init* is a configuration file named aspirate. json. Primarily, it stores answers to the questions you were asked to configure the building of images and the pushing of them to registries.

There is a lot of functionality built into *aspirate*. It's capable of building container images, pushing them to registries, generating Kubernetes manifests and kustomization files, and even deploying your system to Kubernetes. It's also under active development (at the time of writing), so there could be a lot more and many changes in the future.

I'll show an example of a quick Kubernetes deployment, using a cluster on my workstation and taking some shortcuts to try to keep the demonstration simple and without requiring a broad knowledge of Kubernetes (though knowing a little about Kubernetes is probably required to really understand this).

First, I'll create a Kubernetes cluster locally using the kind (Kubernetes in Docker) tool. This is a handy and convenient utility that can create disposable clusters on a workstation using docker containers as the nodes in the cluster. The quick start in the kind documentation has installation instructions (https://kind.sigs.k8s.io/docs/user/quick-start/).

With kind installed, I can create a cluster using

```
$ kind create cluster -name aspirate
```

This gives me a cluster to work with and sets my current context to use this cluster. You can confirm this with the Kubernetes command-line interface, *kubectl*. Docker Desktop (on Windows and Mac) provides a version of kubectl, so there's a good chance you already have it. If not, there is good documentation for getting it (https://kubernetes.io/docs/tasks/tools/).

```
$ kubectl config get-contexts
CURRENT NAME            CLUSTER         AUTHINFO      NAMESPACE
*       kind-aspirate kind-aspirate   kind-aspirate
```

Ideally, before moving into .NET stuff, I'd set up a container registry where I can push my images when I build them and where my cluster can get them to create containers to run pods. I certainly can do that locally, simply with a docker container from the image *registry registry:latest*, but there are some complications to making this work smoothly. The trouble is that I'd need the registry to have a location accessible both from my machine and from inside the cluster, which is a little trickier than it sounds. *localhost* has a different meaning when referenced directly from my terminal than it does inside the cluster. There are ways around this like setting up a hosts file to resolve to a name I can use and/or configuring the node containers in the cluster to resolve a name, but all of this takes away from the focus of what we're trying to do here, so I'll take what I think is a simpler shortcut for making the images available to the cluster after creating the images. In short, I'll not mess with creating a registry for the purposes of this demo. Please understand that in most cases, you'll want to push container images to a registry in order to use them in a Kubernetes cluster, which will pull them from the registry.

After creating a project with .NET Aspire and building images, getting images available to my cluster, and creating manifests with aspirate, I'll be able to deploy to it. This makes the next step that I'll create a new simple system using .NET Aspire to get the ball rolling.

```
$ dotnet new aspire-starter --use-redis-cache -o Demo.Aspirate
```

I'll turn this into a Git repository, add a *.gitignore* file, and create a commit to make it easy to see what happens when I run *aspirate* commands.

```
$ cd Demo.Aspirate
$ git init
$ dotnet new gitignore
$ git add .
$ git commit -m "New system to demonstrate aspirate"
```

Having already installed aspirate (and included the dotnet global tools directory in my PATH), I can now initialize it for my system. To do so, I'll first need to be in my AppHost project's directory.

```
$ cd Demo.Aspirate.AppHost
```

Note   I like to run commands from my solution directory because I can avoid having to change directories frequently and looking at results of *git status* make more sense to me when I look from the same location consistently. aspirate does support a *–project-path parameter* to enable running from a directory other than the AppHost project directory. It would generally be my preference to use this, but I have had results doing that that are not completely favorable with aspirate sometimes not being able to find generated files where it expects. This is a consequence of using a project still under active development and working out the kinks. Because I get better results by changing to the orchestration project directory, I'll recommend doing that, at least with aspirate and at least in its relatively early life.

From this directory, we're ready to initialize.

```
$ aspirate init
```

Note that you can give the *init* command parameters, including *–non-interactive* to have it run without asking you a series of questions. This is especially useful in pipeline scenarios where you might want generation of manifests and more without having a human answering the questions. For this demo, though, I'm just letting it ask me for the inputs it needs, especially because I want to build my images without a registry, which is not supported in noninteractive mode (at least at the time of writing).

For the purposes of this demonstration, the questions, my answers, and additional output look like this:

```
(✓) Done: Set 'Container builder' to 'docker'.
Aspirate supports setting a fall-back value for projects that
have not yet set a 'ContainerRegistry' in their csproj file.
Would you like to set a fall-back value for the container
registry? [y/n] (n): n
Aspirate supports setting a repository prefix for all for
projects.
Would you like to set this value? [y/n] (n): y
Please enter the container repository prefix to use as a fall-
back value: demoaspirate
(✓) Done: Set 'Container repository prefix' to 'demoaspirate'.
(✓) Done: Set 'Container fallback tag' to 'latest'.
Aspirate supports setting a custom directory for 'Templates'
that are used when generating kustomize manifests.
Would you like to use a custom directory (selecting 'n' will
default to built in templates ? [y/n] (n): n
(✓) Done: Configuration for aspirate has been bootstrapped
successfully at 'Demo.Aspirate.AppHost/aspirate.json'.
```

Note that the first line of output didn't ask a question at all and just informed me that aspirate is using Docker for building the images. This is a perfectly reasonable default and I'm happy with it.

The net result of this command is the creation of a new file, which can be confirmed with

```
$ git status
On branch main
Untracked files:
  (use "git add <file>..." to include in what will be
  committed)
        Demo.Aspirate.AppHost/aspirate.json
        nothing added to commit but untracked files present
        (use "git add" to track)
```

The contents of this file essentially save the answers I gave to the *init* command to save my preferences for how I want to generate my images.

```json
{
  "TemplatePath": null,
  "ContainerSettings": {
    "Registry": null,
    "RepositoryPrefix": "demoaspirate",
    "Tags": [
      "latest"
    ],
    "Builder": "docker",
    "BuildArgs": null,
    "Context": null
  }
}
```

You may be well served to commit this file to your repository to share with your team so everyone is using a standard configuration and won't need to answer these questions. You may not want to have developers pushing to a common registry, though, while testing different changes, so if you configure a registry, you might not want that committed. You'll have to decide whether this configuration should be shared with your team or included in a .gitignore to avoid that.

After initialization, there are several commands we can use with aspirate. *run* and *stop* are useful for just running your system in one go and stopping that same running system, respectively. They are useful for typical developer experience workflows.

I'll focus, though, on the more granular commands *build*, *apply*, and *destroy* to take a closer look at what aspirate is really doing.

First, we can use the build (and push) container images for the processes in our system. Many systems will include images you don't need to build, like images for database systems or other dependencies you're pulling down from public registries. Those are not getting built in executing this command, but the .NET and other projects (like Node or Python projects or Dockerfiles explicitly included in your app model) in your system will be built, both in terms of building binaries from your projects and in terms of creating container images to run those resulting processes.

Because I have chosen not to use a container registry, instead of pushing the resulting images to the desired registry, I'll just have the resulting images locally on my workstation to be referenced by my running Docker instance.

The *build* command, like all of the other commands, can be run in noninteractive mode, but does ask for input by default and if the input is not given as arguments to the command. With my current configuration, I can do a simple build.

```
$ aspirate build
```

This command, given the way I configured with *init*, asks me two questions. One is for a password for encrypting secrets, and the other is which of my projects do I want to include in building. Most of the time, the answer to the latter question is *all of them*, but there are certainly times when it might be expedient to limit what you're building. The former question is because aspirate has support for encrypting secrets such that it will hold onto them encrypted and ask for the same password to be able to decrypt for deployment. You can opt out of having aspirate manage secrets with *–disable-secrets*, but I've here just given it a password that I'll remember for when I deploy. The build command, after the questions are asked and answered, will show output indicating that it built the projects and built the images.

For me, that output looks like

```
── Handling Configuration ─────────────────────────────────
Successfully loaded existing aspirate bootstrap settings from '.'.

── Handling Aspire Manifest ───────────────────────────────
Generating Aspire Manifest for supplied App Host
(✓) Done:  Created Aspire Manifest At Path: /home/raelyard/
code/play/aspire-book-code/Demo.Aspirate/Demo.Aspirate.AppHost/
manifest.json

── Selecting Required Components ───────────────────────────
Processing all components in the loaded file, as per the
state file.

── Gathering Information about deployables ─────────────────
Gathering container details for each project in selected
components
(✓) Done:  Populated container details cache for project
apiservice
(✓) Done:  Populated container details cache for project
webfrontend
Gathering Tasks Completed - Cache Populated.

── Handling Projects ──────────────────────────────────────
Building all project resources, and pushing containers

Executing: dotnet publish "/home/raelyard/code/play/aspire-
book-code/Demo.Aspirate/Demo.Aspirate.AppHost/../Demo.Aspirate.
ApiService/Demo.Aspirate.ApiService.csproj" -t:PublishContainer
--verbosity "quiet" --nologo -r "linux-x64" -p:ContainerReposit
ory="demoaspirate/apiservice" -p:ContainerImageTag="latest"
```

```
(✓) Done:  Building and Pushing container for project
apiservice
```

```
Executing: dotnet publish "/home/raelyard/code/play/aspire-
book-code/Demo.Aspirate/Demo.Aspirate.AppHost/../Demo.Aspirate.
Web/Demo.Aspirate.Web.csproj" -t:PublishContainer –verbosity
"quiet" --nologo -r "linux-x64" -p:ContainerRepository=
"demoaspirate/webfrontend" -p:ContainerImageTag="latest"
(✓) Done:  Building and Pushing container for project
webfrontend
Building and push completed for all selected project
components.
```

```
── Handling Dockerfiles ────────────────────────────────
No Dockerfile components selected. Skipping build and
publish action.
```

We can confirm that the images were built by asking docker to show container images available on the local workstation.

```
$ docker image ls
REPOSITORY                                  TAG
demoaspirate/webfrontend                    latest
demoaspirate/apiservice                     latest
```

Note   Earlier versions of Docker listed images with the *docker images* command and running containers with *docker ps*. They later unified the API to make it more consistent by favoring *docker image ls* and *docker container ls*. The older commands are still supported. If you're used to seeing and using *docker images*, please don't be confused by what I used here. It's the same thing.

Recall that I chose not to use a registry, so there is no registry prefix indicated for these images. They do, however, have the prefix I configured with aspirate to put into the repositories for output images. I chose not to use a registry because it would be more trouble to deal with making my registry accessible in my cluster than it would be worth (for the purposes of this demo – in your real systems, you very likely do want to have a local registry to play with if you do deployment to a local cluster as a part of your testing and development efforts).

Now, I'll load my images into the node serving my cluster. This is the shortcut I'm using instead of pushing the image to a registry. I used kind to create my cluster and I'll use it again to preload these images. Again, you'd typically push images to a registry accessible to the cluster, but this is just a trick to avoid having to get a registry set up in my local environment. Kind offers the ability to load an image onto the node(s) container(s) supporting the test cluster. I'll do that for both of the images we just built with aspirate.

```
$ kind load docker-image demoaspirate/webfrontend:latest
--name aspirate
Image: "demoaspirate/webfrontend:latest" with ID "sha256:fbbe
c0114ec381c4438acb82207b80f567807015716d6dc0ecaa8cad32d35d0f"
not yet present on node "aspirate-control-plane", loading...
$ kind load docker-image demoaspirate/apiservice:latest
--name aspirate
Image: "demoaspirate/apiservice:latest" with ID "sha256:3398f6f
f255c0867236d07653b060d593f64929a9307112362ad2ed3afb4bf15" not
yet present on node "aspirate-control-plane", loading...
```

What this has accomplished is that now, these images are present on the only node in this cluster and so, as long as the manifests referencing these images do not use a pull policy of *Always* (which means the cluster will try to pull the image from a registry every time it tries to create a container from it to support a pod), it will find the image already present and just use it.

Note   This is not a trick you'd want to try to use anywhere except on a local development workstation, and using kind wouldn't make sense anywhere but on a kind cluster you'd only be using for testing anyway.

So now we've modeled a system using .NET Aspire and built images to support it using aspirate (which, in turn, used Docker). We're not done yet. The next step is to use aspirate to generate the manifests we need to deploy to Kubernetes.

Before we turn our attention, though, to generating manifests, let's look at what has changed on the filesystem. Recall that *aspirate init* created a configuration file on the filesystem. Two more files have been generated by *aspirate build*.

```
$ git status
On branch main
Untracked files:
  (use "git add <file>..." to include in what will be
  committed)
        aspirate-state.json
        aspirate.json
        manifest.json
```

One of these files was created by .NET Aspire, as directed by aspirate and the other by aspirate itself.

manifest.json is the .NET Aspire manifest. I'll say a bit more about it in a section about the manifest itself. For now, know that it's a JSON document generated by .NET Aspire that articulates the information a deployment tool needs to know to deploy your system. The *azd* Azure Developer command-line interface tool uses this output of Aspire to construct Bicep documents to deploy an Aspire-based system to Azure, leveraging Azure

Container Apps, and aspirate uses it to know container images it needs to build and to generate Kubernetes manifests. As this file is generated from your app model, you probably don't want to commit it to your repository and would be well served to include it in your .gitignore file. Your team may have a different preference, but that's a good default.

aspire-state.json is a file created by aspirate to persist your input to how you want it to build, generate, and apply. Keeping this file affords you the opportunity to just use it to prevent needing to answer the same questions repeatedly as you work with aspirate. Like the aspirate.json file, you may or may not want this in source control and you may or may not want it in your .gitignore.

The next step in deploying this simple distributed system is to generate the manifests we need to deploy it. For that, we'll use *aspirate generate.*

Note   Aspirate supports generating output in the form of simple Kubernetes manifests, Kubernetes manifests with kustomization files, Helm charts, and Docker Compose files. It defaults to manifests with kustomization files and I'll just use that here but be aware that it has the flexibility of doing more that may better fit what you need to do and/or it may be useful to you to generate different outputs for different uses.

By default, *generate* will first build and then generate the requested output. If you have already done the build step, you don't need to do it again. This is similar to *dotnet build* implicitly restoring packages before building or *dotnet test* implicitly building (and therefore restoring) before executing tests. To bypass the build step, you can use *–skip-build*. If you don't use that option, the images will be built again (which does take a finite amount of time.

```
$ aspirate generate --skip-build
```

Generate will also ask a series of questions, which can be bypassed by providing parameters and using noninteractive mode instead. Among these questions, it will ask if you want to use the state file or provide new answers to the questions already answered in the build step.

It also asks for the password for the secrets and you'll need to give the same password for it to be able to decrypt the secrets to proceed. Additionally, it will ask if you want to deploy the Aspire dashboard and connect the telemetry from your system to it. Running aspirate in pipelines, you might answer *no* to this and set up sending your information to your OpenTelemetry endpoint of choice, but I'll say *yes* for this demonstration to be able to see the dashboard in my test cluster.

Another question will be about the image pull policy you want to use. The options are IfNotPresent, Always, and Never, with IfNotPresent the default selection. There are good reasons you might want to use Always when you are deploying resources to your real clusters, but with my test cluster using kind and not using a registry, a pull policy of Always would mean that the cluster would not create a container using our images unless it first pulled them from a registry and it would fail every time it tried to pull for the registry I did not set up. For this reason, you must use an option other than Always if you're getting the image in the cluster the way I did. I'll use IfNotPresent.

Further, it will ask if you want to deploy all the manifests in a custom namespace. It's my preference to say yet to this. For deploying to real clusters, though, you may not want explicit namespaces in the manifests and instead you'll specify a namespace at apply time. This is especially true if you are installing the same set of resources into more than one namespace. For example, you might have a cluster serving more than one environment and install into a different namespace for each environment. Here, I'll just have it use a namespace of *demoaspirate*.

Lastly, it asks if you want to generate a top-level kustomize manifest to run against your cluster. I'll say *yes* to this as well. This will lead to generation of a file that references the other resources and a single point to enable deploying the whole system, including the dashboard. This is necessary to proceed to the next step I'll do here, which is to apply the generated manifest package to the cluster using *aspirate apply*.

Before we move on to applying, though, let's examine the output directory to see what the *generate* command created.

If you, like me, took the default location for output, you should see a directory called *aspirate-output* (as a subdirectory of your AppHost project directory). In it, you should find YAML files called *dashboard.yaml*, *kustomization.yaml*, and *namespace.yaml* in addition to subdirectories named apiservice, cache, and webfrontend.

If you are familiar with Kubernetes manifests and Kustomize, the contents of these files will be familiar to you. If you are not, this book will not cover getting you up to speed on Kubernetes and deploying to Kubernetes. It is, instead, about .NET Aspire and the support for deploying with Aspire. There is overlap in these topics, but you can find many resources for learning more about Kubernetes.

The subdirectories also contain YAML files that are a mix of Kubernetes manifests and kustomization files. The net result is a set of namespace, deployment, and service resources ready to be deployed to Kubernetes. For deploying to real clusters in your canonical environments, you'll have more to think about, but for our purposes of just deploying to a local test cluster, we're ready to let aspirate do that for us.

Note   As of the time of writing, aspirate does not include ingress resources in the manifests, but there is an open issue on the repository and thought is being put into what it might look like. When you read this, it may already be handled (`https://github.com/prom3theu5/aspirational-manifests/issues/85`).

Applying my generated manifests to my cluster is as easy as

```
$ aspirate apply
```

This asks again for whether I want to use the prior state and prompts for the password for secrets. It also asks if I'd like it to read my kubeconfig and choose a context to deploy to. On answering yes, it shows me my contexts and I choose the one I set up for this purpose (*kind-aspirate*, which was generated by kind when I created the cluster with the name *aspirate*). Upon completion of the questions, aspirate gives me output showing it has applied the set of resources defined by the *generate* step.

—— Handle Deployment to Cluster ————————————————————

```
Executing: kubectl apply --server-side -k /home/raelyard/code/
play/aspire-book-code/Demo.Aspirate/Demo.Aspirate.AppHost/
aspirate-output against kubernetes context kind-aspirate.
namespace/demoaspirate serverside-applied
configmap/apiservice-env serverside-applied
configmap/cache-env serverside-applied
configmap/webfrontend-env serverside-applied
secret/webfrontend-secrets serverside-applied
service/apiservice serverside-applied
service/aspire-dashboard serverside-applied
service/cache serverside-applied
service/webfrontend serverside-applied
deployment.apps/apiservice serverside-applied
deployment.apps/aspire-dashboard serverside-applied
deployment.apps/cache serverside-applied
deployment.apps/webfrontend serverside-applied
(✓) Done: Deployments successfully applied to cluster 'kind-
aspirate'$
```

When I created the cluster with kind, it set my current context to the same one I configured for aspirate to apply to, so I can use the Kubernetes command-line interface (kubectl) to confirm I see the resources I expect in the cluster in the namespace I gave.

```
$ kubectl get all --namespace demoaspirate
NAME                                      READY   STATUS
RESTARTS    AGE
pod/apiservice-57f6dfc8b-sjv5w            1/1     Running
0           36m
pod/aspire-dashboard-5777897887-mqs68     1/1     Running
0           36m
pod/cache-69754b6b9c-m4rld                1/1     Running
0           36m
pod/webfrontend-b59cf7ff6-7dmxb           1/1     Running
0           36m

NAME                        TYPE         CLUSTER-IP
EXTERNAL-IP    PORT(S)                 AGE
service/apiservice          ClusterIP    10.96.179.249
<none>         8080/TCP,8443/TCP       36m
service/aspire-dashboard    ClusterIP    10.96.110.252
<none>         18888/TCP,18889/TCP     36m
service/cache               ClusterIP    10.96.250.225
<none>         6379/TCP                36m
service/webfrontend         ClusterIP    10.96.105.232
<none>         8080/TCP,8443/TCP       36m

NAME                               READY   UP-TO-DATE
AVAILABLE    AGE
deployment.apps/apiservice         1/1     1
1            36m
deployment.apps/aspire-dashboard   1/1     1
1            36m
```

```
deployment.apps/cache                    1/1      1
1             36m
deployment.apps/webfrontend              1/1      1
1             36m
```

NAME	DESIRED	CURRENT
READY AGE		
replicaset.apps/apiservice-57f6dfc8b	1	1
1 36m		
replicaset.apps/aspire-dashboard-5777897887	1	1
1 36m		
replicaset.apps/cache-69754b6b9c	1	1
1 36m		
replicaset.apps/webfrontend-b59cf7ff6	1	1
1 36m		

Success! We've now defined a system, built binaries and images, sneaked the images into a cluster, generated deployment manifests, and deployed to a local test cluster. Note that we have created four Kubernetes deployment resources for this system. Only two of these are the application processes for which we are responsible for the code (apiservice and webfrontend). The other two are aspire-dashboard and cache, which is the Redis instance serving our cache. The *cache* deployment is interesting because it was provided for use by simply giving the *–use-redis-cache* parameter to exercising the *dotnet new* template for the aspire-starter solution. This, in turn, included the Redis cache integration into our system, and this resulted, ultimately, in a running deployment in our cluster. This is a pretty remarkable achievement, when you think about it.

To verify that we can reach into our cluster and see the running deployment, we can forward a port to make it available to our workstation from the cluster.

```
$ kubectl port-forward service/aspire-dashboard --namespace
demoaspirate 18888
```

This enables directing my browser to http://localhost:18888 to see the Aspire dashboard, running in my cluster, complete with the structured logs, metrics, and traces I've come to expect.

Figure 7-6. *.NET Aspire dashboard, running in a Kubernetes cluster, deployed there by Aspir8, showing structured logging from a system using Aspire*

I can also forward a port to see the web frontend application functioning fully.

```
$ kubectl port-forward service/webfrontend --namespace
demoaspirate 8080
```

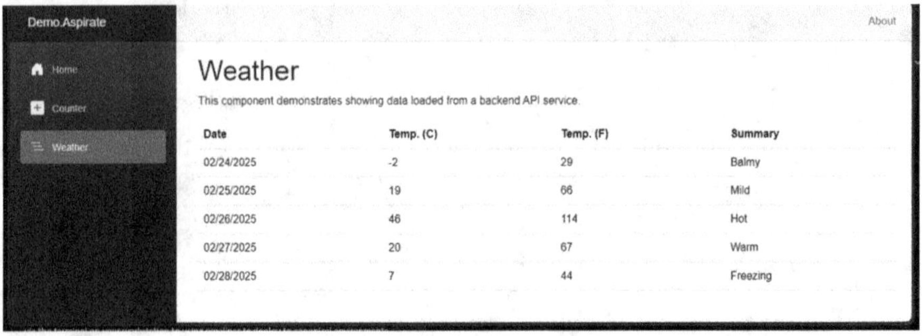

Figure 7-7. *A web frontend resource from a system built with .NET Aspire, running in a Kubernetes cluster, deployed there by Aspir8*

This proves the web frontend process in the cluster can talk to the apiservice process in the cluster successfully. I can also refresh the page and note that I see the same response multiple times while the web frontend is serving from the cache and then a different response after a few seconds when the cache expires. This system, running in the cluster, runs as it did by just running the app host on my machine.

Obviously, there is more to think about as you move from deploying to a test cluster via the terminal on your workstation to using pipelines to deploy to canonical environments. This will give you a start, though, on seeing what is possible. Generation of the files that specify Kubernetes resources is a great start, and the aspir8 project is a valuable contribution. I'm fond of GitOps and I suggest that if you're looking into how to deploy to Kubernetes clusters, it's worth giving Argo CD and/or Flux CD a look. Using these GitOps tools, deployment to your cluster becomes a pull model, rather than push with a controller running in a cluster watching a Git repository for updates. With a model like this, you can commit your generated manifests to a repository (perhaps the same one as with your Aspire system, perhaps in a repository in a chain of submodules in a multirepo setup, or perhaps in yet another repository altogether). Commits updating manifests, charts, etc., can be done by pipelines doing generation and then maybe some customization. Saying more about GitOps would not fit within the context of this book about .NET Aspire, but if you want to find out more, the documentation for Argo CD is a good place to start (`https://argo-cd.readthedocs.io/en/stable/`).

The options are limitless, and you are at liberty to cook something up that works for your situation.

Customization of Your Deployment

If your deployment target is something other than Kubernetes or Azure Container Apps, you have some options for the provision of resources and the building and deployment of your application code.

One of those options is to code it yourself from scratch. It's likely, in a system you created before using .NET Aspire, you're already doing this. Your Infrastructure as Code might take the form of using Terraform or Pulumi, which are both Infrastructure as Code tools that use a provider model and work across many clouds and services. You might instead be directly creating ARM (Azure Resource Manager), Bicep, or CloudFormation templates. These are formats specific to cloud providers for defining resources in repeatable ways (the first two are for Azure and the third for Amazon Web Services). Your deployments are likely happening via pipelines in something like GitHub Actions, Azure DevOps Pipelines, GitLab CI/CD, Jenkins, JetBrains TeamCity, or one of the numerous products dedicated to continuously building, testing, scanning, and deploying your applications and systems. Perhaps you're using GitOps, with something like Argo CD or Flux CD.

189

These are all great and sophisticated tools, and if you already have all of this in place, you probably don't need to change that because you are using .NET Aspire. Aspire will enhance your developer workstation experience, and you don't need to change anything else.

There are likely some simplifications you can do to some of your processes, though. Using something like Aspir8 could replace some manual creation of Helm charts, kustomization files, or other forms of Kubernetes manifests with the way it generates for kustomize. Aspir8 supports using manually written Dockerfile(s) if you have them and leverages container building capabilities in .NET if you don't.

Further, the prior section on Aspir8 mentioned that it was creating an "Aspire manifest." This is because Aspire, itself, supports the creation of a manifest document, articulating the elements of the distributed system based on its app model. This is not something specific to aspirate, but rather a native output format supported by .NET Aspire. Your app model can be turned into a manifest that you can use to generate whatever you need, similarly to how Aspir8 is doing that very thing.

The .NET Aspire Manifest

You can instruct the dotnet CLI to produce the Aspire manifest directly by using

```
$ dotnet run --publisher manifest --output-path manifest.json
```

Note   The above command works directly in the directory of the AppHost project. If you are elsewhere, like at the solution root directory, you'll need to specify the AppHost project directory with the *--project* parameter. Your app model can be turned into a manifest that you can use to generate whatever you need, similarly to how Aspir8 is doing that very thing.

Using the demonstration project I used with showing Aspir8, I get a manifest that looks like this:

```
{
  "$schema": "https://json.schemastore.org/aspire-8.0.json",
  "resources": {
    "cache": {
      "type": "container.v0",
      "connectionString": "{cache.bindings.tcp.host}:{cache.bindings.tcp.port}",
      "image": "docker.io/library/redis:7.4",
      "bindings": {
        "tcp": {
          "scheme": "tcp",
          "protocol": "tcp",
          "transport": "tcp",
          "targetPort": 6379
        }
      }
    },
    "apiservice": {
      "type": "project.v0",
      "path": "../Demo.Aspirate.ApiService/Demo.Aspirate.ApiService.csproj",
      "env": {
"OTEL_DOTNET_EXPERIMENTAL_OTLP_EMIT_EXCEPTION_LOG_ATTRIBUTES": "true",
        "OTEL_DOTNET_EXPERIMENTAL_OTLP_EMIT_EVENT_LOG_ATTRIBUTES": "true",
        "OTEL_DOTNET_EXPERIMENTAL_OTLP_RETRY": "in_memory",
        "ASPNETCORE_FORWARDEDHEADERS_ENABLED": "true",
        "HTTP_PORTS": "{apiservice.bindings.http.targetPort}"
```

```
      },
      "bindings": {
        "http": {
          "scheme": "http",
          "protocol": "tcp",
          "transport": "http"
        },
        "https": {
          "scheme": "https",
          "protocol": "tcp",
          "transport": "http"
        }
      }
    },
    "webfrontend": {
      "type": "project.v0",
      "path": "../Demo.Aspirate.Web/Demo.Aspirate.Web.csproj",
      "env": {

"OTEL_DOTNET_EXPERIMENTAL_OTLP_EMIT_EXCEPTION_LOG_
ATTRIBUTES": "true",
        "OTEL_DOTNET_EXPERIMENTAL_OTLP_EMIT_EVENT_LOG_
        ATTRIBUTES": "true",
        "OTEL_DOTNET_EXPERIMENTAL_OTLP_RETRY": "in_memory",
        "ASPNETCORE_FORWARDEDHEADERS_ENABLED": "true",
        "HTTP_PORTS": "{webfrontend.bindings.http.targetPort}",
        "ConnectionStrings__cache": "{cache.connectionString}",
        "services__apiservice__http__0": "{apiservice.bindings.
        http.url}",
        "services__apiservice__https__0": "{apiservice.
        bindings.https.url}"
      },
```

```
      "bindings": {
        "http": {
          "scheme": "http",
          "protocol": "tcp",
          "transport": "http",
          "external": true
        },
        "https": {
          "scheme": "https",
          "protocol": "tcp",
          "transport": "http",
          "external": true
        }
      }
    }
  }
}
```

You'll notice that this generated JSON document is composed, at the root, of properties for the schema and the resources of the system. Each property of the *resources* node is a resource defined in my app model. There's a resource called "cache" of type "container.v0" with a property defining what image should be used for the container, in addition to resources of type "project.v0" for the .NET projects. This is essentially a JSON translation of the app model I created in C#.

The .NET Aspire manifest format is well documented and what you do with it is up to you. Using tools like *azd* and *aspirate*, if they fit your needs, is a great way to get a quick start on deployment. If you need to generate something custom to deploy your system, the manifest is a great place to start. You can find the documentation and learn more here: `https://learn.microsoft.com/dotnet/aspire/deployment/manifest-format`.

Summary

The main purpose of .NET Aspire is to ease the difficulty of running software in distributed systems on developer workstations. That doesn't mean it's silent about deployment to environments, both canonical environments and environments on demand.

The app model you create in your app host project in a system using .NET Aspire can be leveraged, in addition to running locally, to produce a manifest describing the resources your system requires. This is good news because tools can consume this manifest to create artifacts to deploy and even directly do deployments on your behalf.

The Azure Developer command-line tool is one such tool. It's able to deploy a system using Aspire to a serverless platform known as Azure Container Apps. This is very easy and very cool. Even if Azure Container Apps is not the ultimate destination where you want to run your software (though it could be), it can be extremely useful as a preview environment for sharing work in progress for review and/or user acceptance testing.

Another tool that makes use of the Aspire manifest is called Aspir8. It produces Kubernetes manifests, including kustomization files and/or Helm charts and/or Docker Compose files to enable deployment to Kubernetes clusters. It is also capable of building container images, pushing them to registries, and getting resources running in a cluster.

Deployed systems need to be monitored and maintained. A part of what .NET Aspire provides is standardization of observability. The next chapter will address observability with systems built with Aspire.

CHAPTER 8

System Observability with .NET Aspire

Nobody likes outages. Software that isn't running properly is a drag for users, support, and software professionals. Keeping systems behaving as expected is critical for the success of any organization. Proper operation of a system depends on understanding what is going right, what is going wrong, and when something needs attention.

Cloud-native software tools enable running at scale and with automation, such that systems can grow to a point of being unmanageable with legacy forms of monitoring and understanding what is happening during operation. With new abilities to create resources with configuration changes and in response to system load comes the need for better ways of staying informed.

Modern software requires more than systems of the past that had manageable deployments of limited numbers of servers. Sprawling cloud deployments can quickly and expensively grow out of control and with little insight into what is happening. Modern deployments require a modern approach to understanding availability, performance, behavior, faults, cost, and utility.

.NET Aspire offers support for using modern tooling for observability. To understand what Aspire has to offer and how to take advantage of it, we'll need to define some terms and look at the landscape of the elements that compose into the broader concern of system observability.

D. Rael, *Getting Started with .NET Aspire*, https://doi.org/10.1007/979-8-8688-1521-8_8

Fundamentals: What Is Observability?

When you think about understanding what is happening in a software system, you probably think about logging, monitoring, metrics, and other terms that might run together a little bit. Sometimes, we use these terms interchangeably and without consideration for why the distinctions matter.

At a high level, observability is a characteristic of a system. A system is observable to the extent that someone responsible for the system can know the state of the system, if something is wrong, and what is wrong if there is something wrong.

Observability is not a binary switch. It's not the case that a system either is or isn't observable. The observability of a system is on a scale of how much understanding is available, how easy it is to access that information, and how it makes the information known.

There is no such thing as perfect observability. You can always improve the observability of your system. In the exercise of supporting a system, you'll need to leverage the observability of the system, and the more observable it is, the more effective you'll be.

Okay, So What Makes a System Observable? (Telemetry)

It's obvious and clear that observability is good and is critical for a successful organization that can support the software it creates.

How to achieve it is a bit more difficult to answer and implement.

Fortunately, a lot of very smart people have been thinking about system observability for a very long time. Common vocabulary and standards have developed around creating information that supports observability. The name given, broadly, to information that supports observability is telemetry.

This means that, while observability is a characteristic of a system, telemetry is information about the system, collected to support the effort of making the system observable. When you operate any system, information about what is happening in the system is telemetry.

Telemetry comes in many forms. You can think about this as information relating to business events happening in the system, technical events happening in a system component, technical characteristics of the resources serving system components, and correlation of pieces of information all resulting from a particular interaction with the system. These forms are often broken down into three categories of information useful for understanding system operation.

These three types of telemetry, logs, metrics, and traces, are known as the "three pillars of observability."

The first form of telemetry is logging. Logs provide information about events that happen in system components. What gets logged is at the discretion of the developers of a system and some logs are better than others. Logs can have too much information, making it difficult to find the information needed in a sea of noise. They can also have too little information such that the necessary insight is unavailable. Good logging within an application process is a subject worthy of book-length treatment on its own. For the purposes of this book, we're interested in the availability of logs from processes, especially in the face of multiple resources running in a scaled out environment. Shipping logs to somewhere they can be used and understood without having to touch every resource in a system is critical in modern software. Readability and queryability of logs are also crucial to the ability to expediently use logged information to identify and take necessary action.

The next form of telemetry is metrics. Metrics are measurements. Metrics can be sourced from logs if the information is quantitative, but they can come from other sources, like (virtual) machine or container characteristics like CPU and memory usage or they can be business indicators like sales volume or something of the sort. The point is that they are quantitative measurements that can be identified to be within expected ranges or not. They might relate to business performance or to some technical measurements.

The final of the three pillars comprising system telemetry is tracing. Traces provide information about the flow of an interaction through a system. The idea is that it's a comprehensive view, slicing through system components and showing a picture of what happened with a given system flow. An example of a system flow might be the handling of a request from a user to a webserver where the website might make a call to an API endpoint, that might interact with a database and maybe enqueue a message that triggers another action in another system component. Viewing this chain of interaction and performance and results is what comprises a trace.

Good telemetry is a necessary prerequisite for a system with good observability. Like observability itself, it's not simple and not binary to say that telemetry is good. Your telemetry, in a well-designed and implemented system, should be adequate to answer the questions you have about the system and to enable notification of anything that needs attention. Telemetry that can support knowing what you need to know is good enough telemetry, and it can always be improved.

The quality of your telemetry is not just about the data themselves, but also about the accessibility of the data for the purposes of understanding the system and identifying anything that needs to be identified.

Availability of Telemetry

Given that it's important that telemetry be available to be useful for providing observability, a framework has emerged called OpenTelemetry. The documentation of OpenTelemetry, at https://opentelemetry.io/, calls it "a framework and a toolkit designed to create and manage telemetry data." It can be thought of as a standard in that it is vendor and tool agnostic and is useful with a variety of sinks to which telemetry data can be sent.

.NET Aspire, by default, makes use of OpenTelemetry as a standard to which it sends telemetry data in the form of logs, metrics, and traces. It does this via the service defaults project. If you look at the project file in a service defaults project, you'll notice references to a lot of packages with names starting with OpenTelemetry. You'll also notice that the default generated *Extensions.cs* class, in the *AddServiceDefaults()* extension method that is the entry point for using service defaults, includes a call to another extension method called *ConfigureOpenTelemetry()*. That function, with one it calls, looks like this:

```
public static TBuilder ConfigureOpenTelemetry
<TBuilder>(this TBuilder builder) where TBuilder :
IHostApplicationBuilder
{
    builder.Logging.AddOpenTelemetry(logging =>
    {
        logging.IncludeFormattedMessage = true;
        logging.IncludeScopes = true;
    });

    builder.Services.AddOpenTelemetry()
        .WithMetrics(metrics =>
        {
            metrics.AddAspNetCoreInstrumentation()
                .AddHttpClientInstrumentation()
                .AddRuntimeInstrumentation();
        })
        .WithTracing(tracing =>
        {
            tracing.AddSource(builder.Environment.
            ApplicationName)
                .AddAspNetCoreInstrumentation()
```

```
                        // Uncomment the following line to enable
                        gRPC instrumentation (requires the
                        OpenTelemetry.Instrumentation.GrpcNetClient
                        package)
                        //.AddGrpcClientInstrumentation()
                        .AddHttpClientInstrumentation();
            });

        builder.AddOpenTelemetryExporters();

        return builder;
    }

    private static TBuilder AddOpenTelemetryExporters
    <TBuilder>(this TBuilder builder) where TBuilder :
    IHostApplicationBuilder
    {
        var useOtlpExporter = !string.
        IsNullOrWhiteSpace(builder.Configuration["OTEL_
        EXPORTER_OTLP_ENDPOINT"]);
        if (useOtlpExporter)
        {
            builder.Services.AddOpenTelemetry().UseOtlpExporter();
        }

        // Uncomment the following lines to enable the Azure
           Monitor exporter (requires the Azure.Monitor.
           OpenTelemetry.AspNetCore package)
        //if (!string.IsNullOrEmpty(builder.Configuration[
        "APPLICATIONINSIGHTS_CONNECTION_STRING"]))
        //{
```

```
//    builder.Services.AddOpenTelemetry()
//        .UseAzureMonitor();
//}

    return builder;
}
```

Note   This is what the code from the template looks like at the time
of writing. .NET Aspire is a fast-moving project that changes quickly,
and what you see may look a little different if you're reading this later.

This code sets up a default export of telemetry that works nicely
with the dashboard and can be routed elsewhere with only changes to
configuration, or with minor code changes. You might further want to
customize in some of your projects how metrics work and what gets
included beyond the default ASP.NET Core instrumentation included here,
but this is a good start.

You might notice some references to configuration settings in this
code. One of these is the setting "OTEL_EXPORTER_OTLP_ENDPOINT".

If you run an app host project and look at the environment variables
in the dashboard in one of your running project resources, you should see
a value for this configuration setting (along with some other settings for
configuring OpenTelemetry). This will direct the output to the dashboard
where you can see logs, metrics, and traces, as we've seen already.

Figure 8-1. *.NET Aspire dashboard showing environment variables
for a project resource making use of service defaults with a value for
exporting telemetry to the dashboard*

The port used by your system will likely be different than mine, but it is injected as an environment variable into the processes started by your app host such that it will just work on your machine.

The dashboard surfaced by the Aspire AppHost is itself an OpenTelemetry server that can receive and aggregate the information coming out of your system components. When we viewed the dashboard in earlier chapters, we saw that the dashboard makes both console log and structured logs available. The difference is that console logs are tailored to reading like a story of system/application operation and structured logs are built as documents with properties that can be queried and aggregated. We also saw that metrics coming out of your running system are available in the dashboard by default.

In your production and nonproduction canonical environments, you'll likely want to use something other than the Aspire dashboard for collecting your telemetry. There are many options for servers that can receive OpenTelemetry, and you can just configure where you want it to go.

Observability Put into Practice

Given that observability is a system characteristic and telemetry is the data supporting observability, there's still something missing. Observability and telemetry are passive – they just are, they don't do.

You need to take action to make your system observability work for you. Really, it's not you that necessarily takes action, but systems as well. Taking action to leverage the observability of your system is known as monitoring. Monitoring modern systems requires modern tools. .NET Aspire helps the monitoring effort by providing support for getting your telemetry into place and pushed to a backend supporting OpenTelemetry such that you can make your system observable. Taking that observability and using it for monitoring completes the chain.

There are many tools for monitoring, some open source, some commercial, and some integrated into cloud providers. Orchestrators like Kubernetes also include support for some forms of monitoring and will consume health checks surfaced by your application, also enabled by .NET Aspire to replace unhealthy resources. Monitoring can take the form of surfacing useful metrics in dashboards, providing alerts when there are problems, and slicing and dicing structured logs and traces.

Summary

Observability is a characteristic of a system that enables knowing what is happening at any given time and what has happened in the past. Telemetry is the information that supports observability. A system can't be observable without the right telemetry. .NET Aspire improves system observability by providing service defaults in the form of extension methods for standardizing how the components of your system collect and share telemetry.

This chapter discussed the nature of observability and how .NET Aspire supports it. The next chapter will dive into creating a new system with Aspire from the start.

CHAPTER 9

Greenfield: Implementing New Systems with .NET Aspire

Greenfield is a term often used to describe the creation of a new project from scratch. This contrasts with brownfield, which refers to working in an existing system, potentially a legacy system.

When you are starting on designing a system from scratch, you are in the enviable position of having unlimited degrees of freedom on your approach. You are also in the unenviable position of having unlimited degrees of freedom on your approach.

What I mean by this is that it's a part of modern culture to value freedom and it feels right that having a landscape full of options is the ultimate in good fortune. In practice, too much liberty without constraints can lead to a paralysis in making decisions and overwhelm in trying to evaluate. It's hard to write on a blank page without some direction, and it's hard to make decisions when every possibility is laid out before you.

© Dave Rael 2025
D. Rael, *Getting Started with .NET Aspire*, https://doi.org/10.1007/979-8-8688-1521-8_9

Building useful software doesn't necessarily mean you'll want to run a distributed system with multiple resources in an environment somewhere other than your workstation. Chances are that you'll, at the very least, want somewhere to persist information and this usually means some sort of datastore.

Even very simple problem spaces often have enough need that you want to be able to model a system in a way you can bring it up and shut it down quickly and easily on your workstation and likely share it with other team members. You'll want them to be able to run the code without fuss and without frustration so they can quickly and effectively contribute.

These desires probably mean using .NET Aspire is a good choice for your approach to design.

Starting Fresh – Where to Begin?

Before you can even think about writing code or laying out solutions and projects, Git repositories, or any other concrete artifacts, you should be thinking about why you are creating your system. "*Why*" is always the foundational question that drives the way everything else comes together.

Input into the question of why the system needs to exist, including the problem you're trying to solve and who will benefit. You need to have an idea of who you are trying to serve and what it would look like to build something successful that meets their needs. You need an idea of the size of the audience and the patterns of how and when and how heavily they might want to use your software.

Many of these questions will not have obvious answers and you'll want to get something in front of users as quickly as possible to get fast feedback as an exercise in discovery that will help you narrow down the possibilities and define what it is you're really trying to do.

However, you can't start without some idea. You can't build anything without an idea of what you're trying to build.

So, you'll think through the probable nature of your creation and design toward something useful at fulfilling your desired ends.

You might give some consideration to whether you will need to have a federation of autonomous services and take an approach like microservices. Unless you already know you need something like that, it's usually best to defer decisions like that and start in one place and move to a more distributed architecture style if you find the need. You might be thinking about whether you use one repository for your whole system or smaller repositories that make up the whole. Again, it's probably best in most cases to start with one place and expand when you find a need. If you do go the route of setting up multiple repositories for different components of your system (that you may or may not call services), it will be useful to refer to Chapter 4 in the section about using .NET Aspire with a multirepo setup.

With your desired ends and early design direction in mind, there will be some common elements of what you'll want to have in any solution.

I have made use of the *aspire-stater* dotnet new solution template in this book to give a picture of what it's like to create a distributed system with .NET Aspire. The reason for this is simple: it's a great way to have some projects and code in front of you to see what you get with Aspire.

I also included the addition of a unit testing project as a sample of what to do when creating a system with .NET Aspire. Unit testing is largely orthogonal to .NET Aspire. You want to do unit testing of your .NET code. You want to build your .NET systems with .NET Aspire. You'll be doing both, but using one does not have much influence on your approach with the other.

For these reasons, fleshing out an app model makes sense in the beginning of creating a system as well as making sure you have a project for unit testing. Additionally, with the support in .NET Aspire for integration testing, you'll want to start with a project where you can run end-to-end tests of your whole running system as well as tests making actual requests and interactions with components of your system.

Generally, I'd not suggest starting with the *aspire-starter* template for building a real system. It creates code you'll probably just delete with all of the weather forecast starter code in the API and Web projects. Also, an API and a Web project depending on the API is a good example of something you might want in your system. Your design will likely look very different, and starting from a new AppHost lets you paint on your canvas without being guided in the direction of the starter. If an API and a website do feel like a good starting point for you and you'd rather delete some files than put together your own solution, you should do what suits you best.

What I would suggest is that you start first with creating a Git repository and writing an initial version of a Readme document, as Tom-Preston-Werner suggested a long time ago: `https://tom.preston-werner.com/2010/08/23/readme-driven-development`.

This gets you started thinking about your system before you start running in directions that may or may not be the right ones. You will also have some words about how to get started with your project that will include what it's like to run on your workstation and where you intend to deploy. You may change your mind later, but all you're doing at this point is thinking and creating something your team can criticize and improve. Only after you've done this do you know what experience you're trying to create when you start putting solutions and projects into your repository.

Turning an Idea into a Project

Now that you have an idea of the developer experience you want, you can start on creating it. This will mean setting up the likes of a package source for private packages and such in addition to creating a solution. Whether you use Visual Studio, the dotnet CLI, or something else, it's straightforward to create a solution and projects. I'd suggest the first projects to put in your solution be for tests, both unit and integration. One project for each. If you have reasons to have more than one project for each, you should do that, but at a minimum, you likely want a unit testing project and a .NET Aspire test project for testing your running system in an end-to-end manner.

Then you want the two foundational .NET Aspire system projects. You'll want to create a service defaults project and an app host project. If you do this before creating test projects, I won't argue with you. For the developer workstation experience, the defaults generated in from the *aspire-servicedefaults* dotnet new template are probably perfect. You'll be able to see your system resources and telemetry in the .NET Aspire dashboard. This is a great start. For environments to which you'll deploy, you probably want to send telemetry somewhere else. You should decide on that at the start of the project. Remember that you've not really created anything until you've deployed it to production, and you haven't really deployed to production until you can observe what is happening in production.

In your app model, you'll be able to start to add resources. This might involve databases, message queues, storage resources, and certainly your code projects. With a Readme, tests, service defaults, an app model, and some starter system resources, you're ready to share your project with a team where team members can get the early-stage system up and running in their own workstation environments. .NET Aspire makes this part simpler than ever before.

In addition to getting a code repository set up, you're going to need environments where you'll deploy. Ideally, this will involve Infrastructure as Code to create the resources you need in your cloud environment (if you're using the cloud). It may be the case that you'll use Azure Container Apps as your deployment target, and you can do something as simple as using your app model as your Infrastructure as Code and just use the Azure Developer CLI (azd) to deploy both your infrastructure and your code. It may be that you need to do something outside your app model to create infrastructure to deploy your assets. Either way, you need to plan what you need, including the planning of what and how many environments you'll need. Consider that in the early stages, you might want to start with fewer environments, even if you think you'll need more and add them as they become necessary. Before you have any users, you might even consider that the only canonical environment you need to start with is production.

Also remember that modern software is not deployed manually from workstations. You want to start with automation that builds, tests, and deploys your software when and where you need it to. This usually means setting up pipelines in the likes of GitHub Actions or GitLab CI/CD or one of any number of such services to build and test your software when you push new snapshots of your code and to create deployable artifacts. Further, you'll want those artifacts to be deployed after they've been created and under the circumstances you define for deeming them ready. The degree to which your organization embraces the ideals of continuous deployment and/or continuous delivery will vary with the needs of those you serve and the constraints you're under.

Automated build, test, and deployment of software is necessary to consider that a project has started. When you have this in place, together with your team able to spring forward into working on the system, you've started on creating something to deliver value.

Summary

New systems are an opportunity to dive into a problem and fully understand it and tackle it in ways that deliver value to end users. It can be an immense challenge to turn nothing into something and requires a thoughtful approach. Building out an app model is a good way to start on creating a system after putting in place some documented thoughts about what the system is and should do and how to get started with running it and creating some vessels to fill with tests that define the way the code should function.

This chapter gives some thoughts on what to think about when approaching a new system. The next chapter will deal with adding .NET Aspire to an existing system to make for a better developer experience and to give some additional options for deployment.

CHAPTER 10

Brownfield: Using .NET Aspire with Existing Systems

Brownfield is a term often used to describe working with existing software. This contrasts with the greenfield work we do in building new systems.

Starting fresh on a new project is exciting and fun and developers love to do it. It's a minority of what we software professionals do, though.

New systems are full of possibility, but existing systems are often full of proof. While you don't necessarily know that a new system is going to succeed or ever be useful to anyone, existing systems are already existing and have continued work on them because they are known to have provided value and there's greater value in sight. It's not universally true that existing systems are valuable, but it's close enough to true to consider it a useful approximation.

Most of the work done on software systems is done on software that does something needed by someone. There are users that care about what the system does and need it to work and work well to accomplish what they seek.

Existing software systems run the world.

Starting on a system with .NET Aspire enables a lot of goodness from the beginning of a project. Adding .NET Aspire to an existing system is also a source of goodness and value and can improve the developer workstation experience and make onboarding of new team members easier.

It's likely on existing systems you've already taken steps to solve some of the problems of working with multiple resources. You might have scripts that do setup, create datastores, and make storage simulators or other resources. You might have Visual Studio configured to run multiple startup projects when you debug or start without debugging. You may have Docker Compose files that create networks, containers, and volumes to make your system run.

Many of these methods of making your system run can be replaced with just using a .NET Aspire app host. It's likely you've put a lot of effort into remediations already and you might lament losing the utility of that effort. There may, though, still be some use for some of what you have already done and, even if not, .NET Aspire can likely give you a better experience. The effort you've put into other methods of solving the same problems is likely, to some extent, what economists call "sunk costs." A sunk cost is already incurred, and there's nothing you can do to get back what you've already expended. Sound reasoning focuses on moving forward from where you are and does not consider the sunk costs that are in the past.

First Things First – Existing Deployments

Before thinking about how to approach adding .NET Aspire to existing systems and how it might improve your developer experience, let's take a moment to think about your deployment of your software as it stands.

It's almost certain that if you have an existing system, you have it deployed somewhere, and you have some methods, processes, and procedures for how and when that happens.

Adding .NET Aspire to your system does not mean you have to change any of that. What Aspire does is add orchestration to your system to make it work seamlessly on your workstation, service discovery that contributes to the same workstation seamlessness, and standard setup to your projects and resources to help you have broad and predictable observability.

The orchestration element can give you some new options for how you deploy, but it does not take away from anything you're already doing. You can continue to deploy as you already do without having to change a thing. .NET Aspire does not get in the way of what you already do.

The service discovery element of .NET Aspire can offer you some ways to simplify your existing methods of configuring how different system components are able to reach and communicate with one another, but not necessarily. You probably already leverage configuration in some form of using environment-specific app settings, private DNS, Kubernetes cluster and namespace DNS, environment variables, or any of many other options for getting the right information in the right place for being able to connect. You might already be using .NET service discovery by way of the *Microsoft.Extensions.ServiceDiscovery* package that is also what .NET Aspire uses. You might be able to simplify what you already have, but what you already have should continue to work as it is, so you don't need to change anything.

The observability element is also something that should continue to work the way you have it. What you are doing for logging, metrics, and traces should not require any change to work in your deployed environments as they always have. Whatever you do for shipping telemetry to wherever it goes will not be broken by the inclusion of .NET Aspire in your system. It could be that you are already using OpenTelemetry, maybe via the same packages referenced by the ServiceDefaults project in a .NET Aspire system. If not, you might consider starting, especially with the ability to just use ServiceDefaults as an easy way to set standards and include them in your processes. You don't have to change anything, though. You might hesitate, though, to immediately add ServiceDefaults and/or you might customize your ServiceDefaults so that it matches the way you observe your system currently. Even if you don't make a move toward using OpenTelemetry globally in all of your environments, you could benefit from just including it on developer workstations to be able to see logs, metrics, and traces from all of your resources in the .NET Aspire dashboard. You could include OpenTelemetry conditionally by looking at the returned value from the *app.Environment.IsDevelopment()* function, as the default generated *Extensions.cs* does for deciding whether to enable the default health monitoring endpoints. You have options.

In short, you do not have to change your deployed environments to start using .NET Aspire. Aspire primarily addresses the developer workstation experience and makes it a lot easier, but you don't have to change how you deploy.

You don't have to change how you deploy, but you might have some new options for how you deploy that you didn't have before when you start to use Aspire in your existing system. The manifest Aspire can generate could be a valuable asset that you could use to generate templates for deployment to cloud providers and/or manifests for deploying to something like Kubernetes. You don't even have to generate these manifests yourself if you leverage Aspir8 or another project that creates useful deployment artifacts. You may or may not be able to use generated resources directly, and you might need to do some modification. They might be useful to you though and might be more expedient than how you're creating those resources now (which might be writing them yourself). The possibilities for what you might do that will fit your needs are limited only by your imagination. Also, that Aspire-based systems can deploy so seamlessly and easily to Azure Container Apps could give you another option.

Why to Add .NET Aspire to an Existing System

When you must run many processes and many types of resources for your system, getting started on a new developer workstation often requires going through a document to perform many steps to get set up.

I have always loved the idea of being able to clone a repository and just run the software. This is a rare phenomenon.

I've worked on projects where getting set up approximated just running because of having scripts in the repository that set up databases and webservers and message queues and more, making the setup a matter of clone, run script, then run.

This is pretty good, but it's not as good as just clone and run. Also, running is usually not as simple as just telling something to run. When running multiple .NET projects that execute as processes, I often found myself either needing to set multiple startup projects in Visual Studio or writing a script to start the many processes running. These both left a lot to be desired because I'd wind up either with several windows with console logs and hunting down the right one to find any desired output was misery or I'd have processes running in the background where it wasn't feasible to look at the output at all or all output from all processes just resulting in noise.

Using containers for the processes is relatively nice, and Docker Compose is great for laying out a system with multiple resources and creating a single starting point to start the whole thing. Console output is contained within the containers and easily accessible any time I want it. There's a lot of goodness in using Compose.

It requires writing a Compose file, though, using a different document structure and adding more YAML to my life. It also needs to build new container images any time I change my application code, and it takes a finite amount of time to do that while I have to wait. Debugging also becomes more complicated as I have to either stop the container and run the process on my machine or use remote debugging in the container which works well with Visual Studio and Visual Studio Code, but it does require doing more.

With .NET Aspire, I can run all my system processes directly on my machine, orchestrated by the app host, without having to wait for imagers to build and containers to start. This is a win. Also, hot reload works, which strongly resembles magic, so it's a clear improvement to the workstation experience. I write the app model in Aspire using C#, so it's the same as what I'm using to write my system. The dashboard just runs and just shows me all of the telemetry I want to see, including structured logs and traces which are not something I'd probably take the time to set up for myself for my workstation.

The dashboard is a powerful development tool with a wealth of information at my fingertips and organized so that I can see individual processes or the whole system as I choose. Debugging is seamless as I can just start the AppHost with the debugger and debug any of the code in my application processes.

If you're using Compose as the way you run your system, you may still have reasons to use your Compose file, but I imagine they will become quite limited when the app host will just run all those things more expediently.

How to Add .NET Aspire to an Existing System

The degree of difficulty in adding Aspire to your system will depend on the complexity of the system. The hardest part is likely writing a useful app model in your AppHost project's Program.cs file. This is where you'll articulate the resources in the system and the dependencies between them.

If you're using a Docker Compose file already, it's a start. You're probably mostly just translating that into an app model.

Writing the app model is probably the hardest part, but it's not the only part. It's also not that hard.

The steps to adding Aspire to an existing system look like the following:

- Create new projects – the AppHost and the ServiceDefaults

- Add references to your ServiceDefaults project in your application process projects

- Call the ServiceDefaults entry extension method (*builder.AddServiceDefaults()*) in the startup of your application process projects in Program.cs

- Call the mapping of health check endpoints in your application process projects at startup in the Program. cs file by calling the app.MapDefaultEndpoints() extension method provided by the ServiceDefaults project in the Extensions class

- Add references to your application process projects in your AppHost project

- Add references to hosting integration packages in your AppHost project

- Write your app model in the Program.cs file

- These steps are all necessary to make Aspire work as it should in your system. Some of them can be combined and simplified by using tooling built into Visual Studio.

If you have an existing solution and you have it open in Visual Studio, you can add .NET Aspire quickly by right-clicking on one of your projects in the solution explorer and expanding the Add menu item to locate the Add menu option for *.NET Aspire Orchestrator Support....*

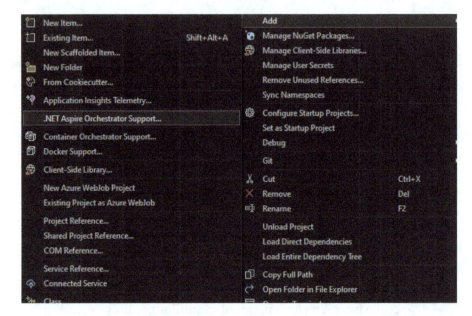

Figure 10-1. *Visual Studio Solution Explorer context menu, "Add" submenu showing option for "Add .NET Aspire Orchestrator Support"*

When you click on this option, you will be presented with a dialog showing that Visual Studio will create projects for your AppHost and ServiceDefaults.

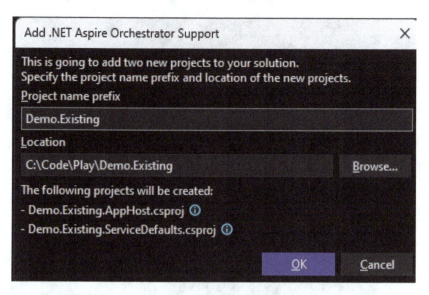

Figure 10-2. *Visual Studio "Add .NET Aspire Orchestrator Support" dialog*

Clicking *OK* will have the desired and expected results. You now have the two new .NET Aspire projects in your solution.

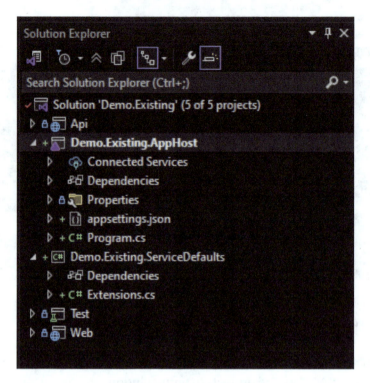

Figure 10-3. *Visual Studio Solution Explorer showing newly added app host and service defaults projects*

Also, the project you right-clicked was already added as a reference to the new AppHost project and included in your app model. In my case, I had done it on the project I named *Api*. Looking at the project file in the AppHost project, I see the reference.

```
<ItemGroup>
  <ProjectReference Include="..\Api\Api.csproj" />
</ItemGroup>
```

The app model in the AppHost's *Program.cs* looks like this:

```
var builder = DistributedApplication.CreateBuilder(args);
builder.AddProject<Projects.Api>("api");
builder.Build().Run();
```

Further, this action updated our existing project as well. The Api project now has a reference to the ServiceDefaults project. You can see this in the Api.csproj project file.

```
<ItemGroup>
<ProjectReference Include="..\Demo.Existing.ServiceDefaults\
Demo.Existing.ServiceDefaults.csproj" />
</ItemGroup>
```

Program.cs in the Api project was updated as well to include the calls to builder.AddServiceDefaults() and app.MapDefaultEndpoints() to hook up the health checks, service discovery, telemetry, and all the goodness of the ServiceDefaults project.

Now add any other application process projects in the solution with the same menu action. Right-click on the project, expand *Add*, and choose *.NET Aspire Orchestrator Support....*

This time the dialog doesn't offer to add projects (because the solution already has the AppHost and ServiceDefaults projects).

Figure 10-4. *Visual Studio confirmation dialog for adding a project to .NET Aspire orchestration*

Just click *OK* here, and the other project (I called mine *Web*) is now included as a reference to the AppHost project and in the app model. In the project file:

```
<ItemGroup>
  <ProjectReference Include="..\Api\Api.csproj" />
  <ProjectReference Include="..\Web\Web.csproj" />
</ItemGroup>
```

In the *Program.cs* file:

```
var builder = DistributedApplication.CreateBuilder(args);
builder.AddProject<Projects.Api>("api");
builder.AddProject<Projects.Web>("web");
builder.Build().Run();
```

The same updates also applied in the Web project as in the Api project. That is, it now references ServiceDefaults and starting up in Program.cs calls both builder.AddServiceDefaults() and app.MapDefaultEndpoints().

This solution is now up and running with .NET Aspire. One remaining item would be to switch to using service discovery. In this example, it's the Web project that depends on being able to make requests to the Api project. To leverage service discovery would require switching from existing configuration for how to find the other project and adding a reference in the app model to enlist in the injection of the right location when running the AppHost.

The Visual Studio tooling makes it easier to add .NET Aspire to your solution that it would be without it, but it's good for you to know what it is doing. These menus and dialogs are compound operations that do a few steps with one invocation that you would have to do sequentially if you were doing them by adding projects one by one.

Note   The C# DevKit extension for Visual Studio Code also brings similar experiences to that editor as well.

Building Out Your App Model

With your projects in place, you're now ready for the fun of making an app model that springs your system to life when you run the app host project. It's handy that Visual Studio assists with this by adding builder. AddProject() calls into Program.cs in the app host, but that's only the beginning. Other resources, like databases, message queue, caches, and storage containers, didn't come along for the ride offered by the orchestration support in Visual Studio. You'll need to make sure to add integration hosting packages to your app host as references and integration client packages to your application process projects. You'll need to build out those resources in the app model and set them up to run the way you desire.

You've seen examples of including Redis and using it for ASP.NET Core output caching and hosting SQL Server and using it for serving data from an API. These are a start on understanding what you need to do to satisfy the dependencies of what your system does. If there's not an integration for what you need, it's likely you can run it in a container. Having an existing system gives you a pretty clear target for knowing what you need to accomplish to get to a running system from an app model.

Summary

This chapter offered some suggestions for why and how to add .NET Aspire to an existing software system. It took a look at some of the additionally nice tools available in Visual Studio and Visual Studio Code.

The next chapter will wrap up what we've learned in this book and assess the state of .NET Aspire and what to look for in the future.

CHAPTER 11

Wrapping Up

Microsoft surprised everyone by introducing .NET Aspire.

Documentation and marketing materials say things like ".NET Aspire is a set of tools, templates, and packages for building observable, production ready apps. .NET Aspire is delivered through a collection of NuGet packages that bootstrap or improve specific challenges with modern app development. Today's apps generally consume a large number of services, such as databases, messaging, and caching, many of which are supported via .NET Aspire Integrations." This is all true and useful, but it's not something you read and feel like saying "Okay, now I have it."

The introduction of Aspire was a pleasant surprise, but it takes some time and effort to understand what it has to offer. It requires still more to get comfortable with using it.

Hopefully this book has helped you on both counts – understanding Aspire and gaining practical knowledge to put it to productive use. We've been through a journey filled with new terms, ideas, concepts, and tools.

We explored .NET Aspire from the perspective of exploring the solution and project template you can use with *dotnet new*.

We discovered the orchestrator in .NET Aspire, the project known as the app host. We used this app host to run distributed systems on workstations. The app host is the place where you create your application model that is the code and builds the composition of your system.

We got to know how Aspire supports production readiness by providing telemetry, health checks, and service discovery with the service defaults project.

© Dave Rael 2025
D. Rael, *Getting Started with .NET Aspire*, https://doi.org/10.1007/979-8-8688-1521-8_11

We explored testing systems and how Aspire helps with that.

We introduced ourselves to .NET Aspire integrations – NuGet packages enabling the enlistment of a broad array of services and resources into our systems via hosting integration packages and client integration packages.

We learned about what .NET Aspire can do to help with deployment of our systems and how it can relate to Infrastructure as Code. Aspire is primarily about the developer experience, but it's a catalyst at the very least for enabling infrastructure provision and software deployment.

We got exposure to the .NET Aspire dashboard and OpenTelemetry.

.NET Aspire Now

After several preview releases, general availability of .NET Aspire was announced on May 21, 2024, with version 8.0 (with major version numbers aligning with .NET releases). The version numbers are tied to .NET versions, but the release schedule is not. .NET uses an annual release schedule for major releases and .NET Aspire releases much more frequently so we can have the latest and greatest the team is cooking up. This is sensible, especially with Aspire so new and still fleshing out a lot of what it has to offer.

At the time of writing, the latest release is 9.1. The current expectation is that releases will ship on a monthly cadence.

The Future of .NET Aspire

The team working on Aspire is filled with outstanding professionals who deliver fantastic software regularly. They are competent folks who are capable of recognizing what is needed and making it happen. Every indication is that .NET Aspire is great as it is now and is just going to continue to get better with more support for more scenarios and types of resources and better capability to just run your software without friction.

Where to Find Out More

To finish this journey together, the last thing I want to leave you with is a list of resources for great information on .NET Aspire.

- .NET Aspire versions and releases: `https://learn.microsoft.com/dotnet/aspire/whats-new/`

- The root of the .NET Aspire documentation with links you can follow all day: `https://learn.microsoft.com/dotnet/aspire/`

- The .NET Aspire GitHub repository: `https://github.com/dotnet/aspire`

- The .NET Aspire samples repository: `https://github.com/dotnet/aspire-samples`

- Aspireify.NET - .NET Aspire news, samples, and tutorials: `https://aspireify.net/`

Index